The Hidden Treasure Within You

A Journey from Darkness to Light

Fathima Amat-ullah

"The love of Allah (ﷻ), The Exalted is a light that, if you are without it,

you are in an ocean of darkness"

Ibn al-Qayyim RA.

INDIA • SINGAPORE • MALAYSIA

Copyright © Fathima Amat-ullah 2024
All Rights Reserved.

ISBN 979-8-89610-812-2

This book has been published with all efforts taken to make the material error-free after the consent of the author. However, the author and the publisher do not assume and hereby disclaim any liability to any party for any loss, damage, or disruption caused by errors or omissions, whether such errors or omissions result from negligence, accident, or any other cause.

While every effort has been made to avoid any mistake or omission, this publication is being sold on the condition and understanding that neither the author nor the publishers or printers would be liable in any manner to any person by reason of any mistake or omission in this publication or for any action taken or omitted to be taken or advice rendered or accepted on the basis of this work. For any defect in printing or binding the publishers will be liable only to replace the defective copy by another copy of this work then available.

Dedication

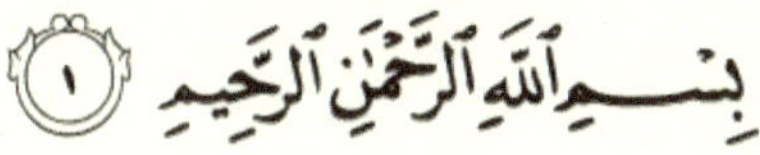

In the name of Allah, the most merciful, the most compassionate.

I begin with my deepest gratitude to My beloved Lord, Allah (ﷻ), The Exalted who guided and helped me to fulfill my long-time dream of completing my book.

The journey of life was never been easy, but I understand His plan was the best of plans and Alhamdulillah for all those Hardships thats one of the reason that has Guided me towards writing this book.

˹He is˺ the One Who created me, and He ˹alone˺ guides me.
˹He is˺ the One Who provides me with food and drink.
And He ˹alone˺ heals me when I am sick.
And He ˹is the One Who˺ will cause me to die, and then bring me back to life.
And He is ˹the One˺ Who, I hope, will forgive my flaws on Judgment Day."
"My Lord! Grant me wisdom, and join me with the righteous.
Bless me with honourable mention among later generations.
Make me one of those awarded the Garden of Bliss.

Quran 26:78 to 26:85

"Enjoy the little things. For one day you may look back and realize they were the big things."

– Robert Brault

Contents

* * *

Introduction

* * *

All praise and thanks are due to Allah (ﷻ), The Exalted. We praise Him and seek His Help, Guidance, and Forgiveness. We seek refuge with Allah (ﷻ) from the consequences of our evil conduct and the sins we have committed. I bear witness that there is no god but Allah (ﷻ) Alone, who has no partner, and I bear witness that Muhammad (May peace be upon him) is His servant and Messenger.

I express my heartfelt gratitude to my beloved parents, Mkc Ismail and Rukhiya Ismail, who always encouraged and believed in me, no matter what endeavour I pursued. I vividly remember the moment I called my mom and told her about my plan to publish a book.

I expected her to question my seriousness, as for years I have been planning and dreaming of it. However, to my surprise, she responded with a heartfelt wish for Allah's blessings for me to complete it.

Alhamdulillah.

My deepest gratitude goes to my little souls, Fathimath Fana, Muhammad Rayyan, and my sweet little pie Amina Aiza, who patiently witnessed me engrossed in long hours of work and never hesitated to bring me a glass of water whenever I needed it. My deepest gratitude to my husband Noushad N. for his unwavering support throughout the journey of finishing my book.

My deepest gratitude to the countless individuals who have inspired me with their unwavering gratitude, especially the prophets, companions, and righteous scholars who have guided humanity towards a path of thankfulness and appreciation. May their stories continue to illuminate our hearts and motivate us to live lives filled with gratitude to Allah, the Most Gracious, the Most Merciful. Their speeches, their words have provided hope and solace through my journey of pain and hardships. My gratitude to my wonderful teachers who helped me throughout my never-ending journey with the Quran, their speech, their advice, their guidance has inspired my words throughout this book. I want to express my gratitude to my wonderful sisters, my colleagues who I share a significant portion of my time with, and my friends who have been my support system during difficult times.

And to the readers, whose hearts are open to the transformative power of gratitude. May this humble offering serve as a testament to the profound impact that gratitude can have on our lives.

We ask Allah (ﷻ) to bestow upon our hearts that which He bestows upon His righteous servants, and the Muslims with the best reward, and gather us with Him at the place of His mercy along with the prophets, the truthful, the martyrs, and the righteous. How excellent the companions are!

Finally, I am grateful to the publishers and editors who have guided this project with expertise and care. Their contributions have been essential in shaping this work into its final form.

To all my wonderful readers, I want to express my deepest gratitude for choosing my book out of the thousands available in stores. I am not an educator or a researcher, nor do I hold any degrees that would qualify me as a genius author. I am just an ordinary working mom, a student of the Quran, a traveller in this world, waiting for the call to return to my Lord, who wants to share the experiences and thoughts in the hopes of bringing a brighter smile to your faces by the end of this book.

This book is for all of you. Whether you are facing pain, broken relationships, illness, physical or emotional challenges, struggles with your children, financial difficulties, or any kind of hardships big or small. It is also for those of you who are experiencing great happiness and abundance in your lives, who have the ability to manifest your desires and enjoy the blessings of health, wealth, and time.

And lastly, this book is for all of us who need gentle reminders to nourish our souls.

This book is not merely an academic treatise on gratitude but a heartfelt invitation to cultivate this invaluable virtue in our daily lives. Through a blend of Islamic principles, insightful reflections, practical guidance, and inspiring stories, we aim to empower readers to embrace gratitude as a path to spiritual growth, a source of resilience, and a key to unlocking the full potential of the human heart.

Within this process of cultivating a grateful mindset, we embark on a journey of self-discovery. By reflecting on our lives and acknowledging the blessings we often take for granted, we gain a deeper understanding of ourselves and our relationship with the Divine. This introspection leads to greater self-awareness, allowing us to identify areas where we can cultivate more gratitude and strengthen our connection with Allah (ﷻ).

Not only social media icons or celebrities can inspire you. It can be the maid at home, the milkman who delivers milk to you, the newspaper boy, the municipal cleaner who keeps the roads clean, the labourers working in the scorching heat, the gardener, the cook who cooks food for you - anyone can come into your life for a brief moment and teach you valuable lessons. The key is to have a receptive attitude to observe and understand things correctly.

I, too, was one of those who didn't notice or reflect much on what was happening around me. Then, I slowly realised that the people you meet, who are placed in your life, whether you like them or not, the words you hear, the conversations that happen - all of it is predestined. Nothing happens without Allah's knowledge. The truth is, we often overlook these signs. Everything in our lives is placed there for a purpose.

I believe we don't meet anyone or any situation by accident. The people you meet or the situations you face have something to teach you - either you learn a lesson or you may be a source to teach them a lesson. But there is a hidden, predestined purpose behind all these moments.

Now, if you are reading these words, this was already predestined. Ponder what our Lord wants you to take away from this moment. What unique lessons can you discover from this book? The hidden wisdom it holds is yours to uncover.

Open your heart, willing to unlearn and relearn, to let go, to flow like water, to soar with light wings. All of this is for you.

This book seeks to remind us that gratitude is not merely a fleeting emotion but a transformative virtue that has the potential to reshape our perceptions, strengthen our resilience, and elevate our lives to a new level of meaning and fulfilment.

I love you all for the sake of Allah, for the mere fact that He has created and chosen you as an honoured race on this earth is reason enough for me to love you all.

"Do not look at Adam but rather see the breath that has breathed into him and be fascinated by it"

– Rumi

Fathima Bint Ismail

Let's start the adventure of the Treasure Hunt!

Interesting right?

It's a beautiful journey, so let's embark on it together. Though many of you may be in different situations right now, let's stay united. We can share our pain, joys, and thoughtful reflections, and ultimately, we can discover the treasure within. I'm sharing my experiences, thoughts, and insights with my wonderful readers, whom I may not have seen, but I can feel your presence connecting with the treasure within me. At the end, as we say goodbye, I trust that each of you will have discovered the treasure inside of you.

"What Hurts you blesses you. Darkness is you candle."

- Rumi

Chapter 1

Alhamdulillah – All praise is due to Allah (ﷻ), The Exalted

* * *

The Profound Significance of "Alhamdulillah": In the Journey of Discovering the Deeper Meaning of Gratitude and Remembrance

The literal meaning of Alhamdulillah is "All praise belongs to Allah." It acknowledges Allah (ﷻ) as the ultimate source of all blessings, both great and small.

Thanks and praise, when we say Alhamdulillah, we are saying that everything we have comes from Allah, and we are grateful to Him for it. No complaints; that was the best to happen at that moment. Nothing better could happen. Nothing at all.

The concept of gratitude in Islamic ethics and spirituality is multifaceted and profound. After praising him, we are also thanking Him for what He has given us. Some may ask, "How's your work today?" "Hmm, okay… Alhamdulillah." If it's hot outside and we say, "It's too hot, I'm sweating," this is not Alhamdulillah; it's a complaint, right?

As a believing Muslim, the first thing to come out of our mouths was Alhamdulillah, it's hot. Alhamdulillah, my work is good. Thanking Him in every situation is a different type of thinking. Alhamdulillah from the bottom of your heart shows that you are grateful for whatever you have. Some Muslims don't understand the true meaning of Alhamdulillah.

The milk spilled out of the pan, and your child broke your glass vase. Please don't panic or shout. Alhamdulillah, the glass vase is broken but your child is safe and didn't get cut. The glass piece could have caused an injury, but thankfully nothing happened. It's okay that the milk spilled, and you didn't get burned. As homemakers, I used to think about this often. We should be grateful to Allah (ﷻ) for his blessings and count them, even if something unpleasant happens because everything that happens to us is for our own good, whether we understand it or not.

I'm usually the one handling the chores.
Woe is me, I'm the one who has to make the meals.
It's my job to teach the kids.
I'm always the one making calls to my family.
Cleaning is my responsibility.
I'm the one who always needs to apologise.
Why me?

Sounds familiar? Many of us, especially women, find ourselves in the role of the "designated worrier", always keeping track of the countless tasks and responsibilities that come with managing a household and a family.

This emotional and mental labour, often invisible and underappreciated, can take a toll on our well-being. However, research suggests that practicing gratitude can help alleviate some of this burden.

Gratitude, the act of acknowledging and appreciating the positive aspects of our lives, has been shown to have numerous benefits. Studies have found that people who regularly express gratitude report higher levels of life satisfaction, stronger relationships, and improved physical and mental health.

In the context of household management, gratitude can help reduce the sense of burden and resentment that often accompanies the "designated worrier" role. When we acknowledge the contributions of our partners or family members, even if they are small, it can help shift the focus away from the tasks we feel responsible for and toward the support we receive.

Even though I used to have these kinds of thoughts, when I shifted my mindset to focus on gratitude, everything changed. I started to say "Alhamdulillah" and realised that everything I'm doing is an opportunity for me to serve my family. Whether it's serving them, apologising, forgiving others, teaching my kids, keeping my house clean, or dedicating myself to my work, I am rising in ranks. Doesn't Allah (ﷻ) love those who do good deeds? Aren't these good deeds? Why did Allah (ﷻ) choose us for the roles we are playing? He trusted us that we could handle it, right? Aren't we special? It all comes down to our thoughts. We can focus on the negatives and complaints, or we can choose to think positively. This change in mindset can make all the difference. Most importantly, Islam encourages the practice of tafakkur and gratitude.

The significance of Alhamdulillah lies in its power to shift our perspective, to elevate our hearts and minds to a state of profound appreciation. It encourages us to move away from focusing on our own desires and shortcomings and to instead fix our gaze upon the endless bounties bestowed upon us by our Creator. This shift in focus leads to a state of contentment and inner peace, allowing us to navigate life's challenges with resilience and grace.

The Quran repeatedly emphasises the importance of expressing gratitude to Allah. In numerous verses, it highlights the blessings that Allah (ﷻ), The Exalted bestows upon us, reminding us to acknowledge these gifts with humility and appreciation. For instance,

In Surah Al-Nahl, verse 18, Allah (ﷻ) says:

If you tried to count Allah's blessings, you would never be able to number them. Surely Allah (ﷻ), The Exalted, is All-Forgiving, Most Merciful.

This verse reminds us of the countless blessings that Allah (ﷻ) has bestowed upon us, blessings that often go unnoticed amidst our daily lives. It urges us to actively seek out these blessings, to recognise them with gratitude, and to acknowledge our dependence on the Divine for everything we have.

Beyond its religious significance, Alhamdulillah holds profound psychological and spiritual benefits. When we practice gratitude, our hearts and minds become more attuned to the beauty and goodness that exists around us. We become more aware of the small joys and blessings that we often overlook. This shift in perspective leads to a greater sense of inner peace, contentment, and overall well-being.

Can anyone easily cultivate the habit of implementing Alhamdulillah in their life? The answer is no. Why? Because it's not easy.

Let me provide an example to Illustrate this point. Consider the case of a farmer. To achieve a good crop yield, the farmer must take numerous measures to ensure success. Cultivating the habit of expressing gratitude through Alhamdulillah is not easy. It requires a concerted and sustained effort, similar to a farmer's work to achieve a successful crop yield.

Consider the example of a farmer. To get a good harvest, the farmer must take many steps. First, they need to choose suitable land with fertile soil, just as we need a clear heart. They must ensure the land is free from pests and insects, like our hearts should be free from complaints and grudges. Choosing the right seeds and timing the sowing process correctly are crucial, just as seeking the right knowledge can clear our hearts from doubts and complaints.

Regularly watering the land and monitoring the crop's growth are essential, akin to engaging in various forms of worship. The farmer must also protect the crop from natural calamities, as we need to safeguard our hearts from distractions and negativity. Even after all this hard work, the farmer must carefully harvest the crop at the right time. Similarly, we need to understand the wisdom behind the knowledge we gain, cultivate gratitude, and maintain a state of trust in Allah (ﷻ) to truly benefit.

Just as the farmer cannot achieve a good crop yield without proper planning and care, we cannot easily cultivate the habit of implementing Alhamdulillah in our lives without a clear strategy and consistent effort.

The power of positive affirmations lies at the heart of cultivating a grateful mindset. Just as a seed planted in fertile ground grows into a strong and vibrant plant, so too do our thoughts shape our reality. When we repeatedly express gratitude, we sow the seeds of positivity and abundance in our hearts and minds. This practice, akin to a gentle yet persistent rain nourishing the earth, fosters a positive outlook that can transform our experiences.

Imagine a barren land, devoid of life and colour. This is a metaphor for a heart burdened by negativity and resentment. Yet, when we introduce the seeds of gratitude, we begin to see a shift. With each "Alhamdulillah" whispered, with each conscious act of acknowledging blessings, we nurture the soil of our hearts. As these seeds take root, they begin to sprout, transforming the barren land into a vibrant garden.

Think about the moments of joy and laughter that brighten your day. The warmth of a loved one's embrace, the comfort of a cosy home, the satisfaction of completing a task, the realisation of a dream, a satisfying food, the water to drink, the oxygen we breathe, the beautiful sky decorated with shining stars, the Sun, day and night – these are all blessings, often fleeting but deeply significant. They are like tiny seeds of happiness sown by Allah, reminding us of His constant care and love.

Even in the midst of challenges, blessings often remain hidden, like diamonds in the rough. When faced with hardship, illness, or loss, it might feel impossible to find gratitude. But Allah's mercy is boundless, and His blessings often manifest in ways we least expect. It's in these moments of struggle that our faith is tested, and our true gratitude is revealed. We learn to appreciate the strength we didn't know we had, the resilience that emerges in the face of adversity. We discover a newfound depth of faith, a connection with Allah (ﷻ) that transcends the boundaries of our comfort zone.

Imagine a ship sailing through a turbulent sea. The storm may be fierce, the waves may crash, but the ship endures, guided by the captain's expertise and the strength of its hull. Allah (ﷻ) is our captain, His wisdom and guidance navigating us through the storms of life. The trials we face are tests of our faith, opportunities to grow closer to Him, and to discover the hidden blessings that await us.

The transformative power of Alhamdulillah is not just about feeling good; it is about aligning our lives with the will of Allah, embracing His blessings, and finding joy in the journey. It is about recognising that every breath, every moment, every experience is a gift, a testament to His. When we truly understand the power of Alhamdulillah, we begin to live a life that is not defined by our circumstances, but by our unwavering gratitude and our unwavering faith in Allah.

Recognising Allah's blessings is a journey that begins with a shift in perspective. It's about training our minds to see the abundant gifts that surround us, both the obvious and the subtle. Just as the sun illuminates the world, providing warmth and life, Allah's blessings illuminate every aspect of our existence.

Remember, the more you focus on the blessings in your life, the more you will notice them. Allah's blessings are like a vast ocean; the more you dip your cup, the more you will find. Embrace a life of Alhamdulillah and allow the

transformative power of gratitude to fill your heart and guide you on a path of purpose and contentment.

From Complaint to Contentment

The journey from complaint to contentment is not a quick fix; it's a gradual transformation of our perspective. Imagine a life where we constantly find ourselves dwelling on what we lack, what's missing, or what we believe we deserve. This constant state of dissatisfaction can leave us feeling drained, resentful, and disconnected from the blessings surrounding us.

This is where the power of "Alhamdulillah" comes into play. When we intentionally shift our focus from what we lack to what we have, a profound shift occurs within us. Instead of dwelling on the negative, we begin to appreciate the abundance already present in our lives. This shift, however, requires conscious effort. It's about making a conscious choice to acknowledge and appreciate even the seemingly small or ordinary things that bring joy, comfort, and purpose to our existence.

Think of it as a gentle redirection of our mental energy. When we choose to express gratitude, we are not simply saying "thank you" to Allah; we are actively rewiring our brains to recognise and appreciate the countless blessings that surround us. Each time we utter "Alhamdulillah," we are reinforcing a positive mental pattern, slowly eroding the negativity and resentment that may have previously clouded our judgement.

Consider the privilege of being able to wake up in the morning, brush your teeth independently, shower on your own, prepare meals, and enjoy a cup of coffee. While we may take these blessings for granted, there are many who are confined to their beds, unable to rise or move independently, unable to walk, hear, see, smell, embrace loved ones, or attend to their basic needs. If someone were to inquire from them:

What if you could make one wish and have it granted?

They would certainly respond, "We hope to have the capability to do things on our own without making it difficult for others to take care of us. We have had the gift of good health and time for many years, but do we truly value it? I doubt, do we?"

Gratitude can also transform how we perceive challenges.

Instead of viewing obstacles as roadblocks or setbacks, a grateful heart sees them as opportunities for growth and learning. Remember, Allah (ﷻ) tests those He loves. When faced with trials, instead of feeling defeated, we can ask ourselves, "What lesson is Allah (ﷻ) trying to teach me through this experience? How can I grow from this challenge?" This shift in perspective allows us to approach adversity with strength and resilience, recognising that even in difficult times, Allah (ﷻ) is guiding and protecting us.

In a world that is obsessed with acquiring wealth and where many believe that money is the key to a successful life, let me share with you the final words of a millionaire on his last moments of life.

Steve Jobs, the co-founder of Apple Inc., is known to many. Many of you must have Apple products in your home or perhaps dream of having one.

By age 25, his net worth grew to an estimated $250 million (equivalent to $838 million in 2023). He was also one of the youngest "people ever to make the Forbes list of the nation's richest people—and one of only a handful to have done it themselves, without inherited wealth."

"I reached the pinnacle of success in the business world. In others' eyes, my life is an epitome of success.

However, aside from work, I have little joy. In the end, wealth is only a fact of life that I am accustomed to.

At this moment, lying on the sickbed and recalling my whole life, I realize that all the recognition and wealth that I took so much pride in have paled and become meaningless in the face of impending death.

You can employ someone to drive the car for you, make money for you, but you cannot have someone bear the sickness for you.

Material things lost can be found. But there is one thing that can never be found when it is lost – "Life".

When a person goes into the operating room, they will realize that there is one book that they have yet to finish reading – "Book of Healthy Life".

Whichever stage in life we are at right now, with time, we will face the day when the curtain comes down.

Treasure Love for your family, love for your spouse, love for your friends...

Treat yourself well. Cherish others.

As we grow older, and hence wiser, we slowly realize that wearing a $300 or $30 watch - they both tell the same time...

Whether we carry a $300 or $30 wallet/handbag, the amount of money inside is the same;

Whether we drive a $150,000 car or a $30,000 car, the road and distance are the same, and we get to the same destination.

Whether we drink a bottle of $300 or $10 wine, the hangover is the same;

Whether the house we live in is 300 or 3000 sq ft, loneliness is the same.

You will realize, your true inner happiness does not come from the material things of this world.

Whether you fly first or economy class, if the plane goes down, you go down with it...

Therefore, I hope you realize, when you have mates, buddies, and old friends, brothers and sisters, whom you chat with, laugh with, talk with, sing songs with, talk about north, south, east, west, or heaven and earth... That is true happiness!

Steve Jobs

Narrated Abu Huraira:
The Prophet (ﷺ) said, "Wealth is not in having many possessions, but rather (true) wealth is feeling sufficiency in the soul."
Ref: Sahih al Bukhari 6446

Chapter 2

Gratitude is an attitude

* * *

The Transformative Power of Gratitude

Scientific research has consistently shown the numerous benefits of practicing gratitude in our daily lives. Studies have found that individuals who cultivate an attitude of gratitude experience an enhanced sense of well-being, greater resilience, and improved emotional and physical health. They may also exhibit higher levels of empathy, optimism, and overall life satisfaction.

As they say, "Gratitude is an attitude,"

As per Oxford, attitude is a settled way of thinking or feeling about something. It means you need to work for it.

To encourage positivity and create a life filled with joy and contentment, it's essential to cultivate an "Attitude of Gratitude." By consistently acknowledging and appreciating both the big and small blessings in our lives, we can enhance our sense of well-being, resilience, and overall quality of life.

The Qur'an instructs us that "if you are grateful, I will surely increase you [in favor]" [14:7]

Gratitude has a significant impact on our physical and mental health. Extensive research has shown that fostering an attitude of thankfulness and appreciation can have profound positive effects on an individual's overall health and well-being. Studies have demonstrated that cultivating gratitude can result in lower blood pressure, improved immune function, increased happiness and life satisfaction, as well as a reduced risk of depression, anxiety, and substance abuse disorders.

If we look into today's world, as per WHO (World Health Organization), more than 720000 people take their own lives every year… can you imagine? Suicide is the third leading cause of death among 15-29-year-olds.

The reasons for suicide are multi-faceted, influenced by social, cultural, biological, psychological, and environmental factors present across the life course. It's a serious public health problem that requires a public health response. As part of the public, how can we help prevent this? As parents, individuals, colleagues, friends, siblings, and children, we can all play a big role.

According to the WHO, the main reason behind suicide is depression. It can happen impulsively in moments of crisis when there's a breakdown in the ability to deal with life stresses, such as financial problems, relationship disputes, or chronic pain and illness.

Today's generations often define success as having a huge bank balance, cars, mansions, and a luxurious life. If so, then why do many so-called "successful" celebrities take their own lives? Didn't they have a huge bank balance, fame, and luxury?

Gratitude, on the other hand, can be a powerful antidote to this crisis. Being grateful and appreciating the good things in life, no matter how small, can improve mental health and well-being.

According to a study, teens who used screens more often were more likely to report higher levels of suicidal ideation, anxiety, and depression. In contrast, studies have found a link between gratitude and reduced suicide risk.

Expressing gratitude has been shown to increase feelings of happiness, life satisfaction, and overall well-being.

Gratitude

It's a potent force that transforms our hearts, shaping our thoughts, words, and actions, leading us towards a deeper understanding of the divine. This journey of gratitude, however, is not merely about appreciating the good times; it's about recognising the divine hand in every experience, even the challenging ones. By cultivating this profound sense of thankfulness, we unlock the doors to contentment, humility, and a profound connection with the divine.

Furthermore, gratitude serves as a powerful antidote to the seeds of discontentment and arrogance that can take root within us. When we focus on the blessings we have been given, we become less consumed by our perceived

shortcomings and desires. This shift in perspective fosters humility, reminding us that we are but humble servants of Allah, constantly in need of His grace and mercy.

Humility, in turn, paves the way for contentment, a state of inner peace that stems from accepting our circumstances and recognising the blessings in our lives. When we focus on what we lack, we create a void that can never be filled, leaving us feeling dissatisfied and restless. Conversely, when we focus on what we have, we create a sense of abundance and contentment, even amidst challenges.

"Success" to me is when your heart is content with what you have. It's when you don't compare yourself to others or envy what they have. Success is also when you teach your children that while money is essential, it's not the only factor that leads to happiness and contentment.

By practicing gratitude, we can shift our focus from what we lack to what we already have. We can appreciate the small moments, the people in our lives, and the simple pleasures that often go unnoticed.

When we teach our children the meaning of true happiness and show them the power of gratitude, our society will witness a significant change.

"Gratitude is something you need to practice; it doesn't happen in a day."

Allah, The Exalted says in The Quran,

"Then remember Me; I will remember you. And be grateful to Me and do not deny Me."

(Quran 2:152)

Gratitude in Times of Difficulty

Every day, life is becoming more challenging. It is important to understand that every person experiences pain and challenges at some point in their life. Is there anyone who can say they have never experienced any pain in their life? Nobody is able to.

In fact, the newborn baby is considered to be healthy when the baby cries, right? In fact, that's the only language they know to communicate their needs. Pains can act as a form of communication, signalling to us the changes that need to be made. Suffering is an unavoidable aspect of existence. Day and night exist. Doesn't the sun come up after a night of darkness? There are peaks and valleys. Are there both summer and winter seasons? When life comes to an end, new lives are born. The trees lose their leaves as a form of rejuvenation. This principle is applicable everywhere. To develop and face new challenges, it is necessary at times to release something.

When we face hardship, negativity can easily cloud our judgement and lead us to despair. However, by consciously choosing to express gratitude, even amidst struggles, we anchor ourselves to a higher perspective. This practice serves as a shield against negativity, helping us to maintain our faith and find strength within ourselves.

According to Ford, plants use the dropping of leaves as the primary way of excretion. Trees send toxic substances such as tannins, oxalates, and heavy metals into the leaf shortly before it drops from the branches. That is pretty convenient. The leaf is shed from the tree and toxic substances that can't be dissolved in water and evaporated through the leaves are carried along with it.

Sometimes we too need to shed our leaves, the toxic thoughts of our heart, so that we can make space in our hearts to allow new leaves of hope to emerge. To be grateful at every moment must be a part of our life.

Now, what makes us truly grateful in these difficult times is having complete faith and hope in our Lord. Let me ask you something to ponder. Whom do you love the most in your life? Answer from your heart, for your heart will never lie to you.

As human beings, we are willing to sacrifice anything for our loved ones. I have witnessed people taking their own lives upon losing the love of what they believed to be their entire world. To take such a drastic step for someone who was only briefly present in their life - how serious a decision that is!

Now, as believers, we often claim that we love Allah(ﷻ). If you and I truly love Him, can any decision the Almighty takes for us be wrong? It's not giving up your life; it's giving up your desires that make you deluded in the fantasy of this world. Realise that nothing in this world truly belongs to us. When you and I recognise this fundamental truth, we will naturally become more grateful.

Let me provide an example. We all claim ownership over our bodies - my hair, my hands, my eyes, my face. But do you know how your heart functions? Do we know the exact number of hair strands we have? Can you stop your hair from falling out? Can you control the blinking of your eyes?

According to the Cambridge dictionary, the meaning of "own" is "belonging to or done by a particular person or thing." If that's the case, then we should know every detail of our bodies, right? But when we feel tired, do we know the exact reason why? No, we need to consult a doctor to identify the cause. Doesn't this make you realise that we don't truly own anything, not even our own bodies?

The only thing we can own and control is our thoughts, and that's a choice given to us by Allah (ﷻ). Now, it's up to us to choose whether to fill our hearts with weeds that can drain the beauty of the roses planted there, or to remove those weeds. The choice is ours.

If you claim to have pure love for our Lord, then consider what you and I are willing to sacrifice. Allah (ﷻ) does not ask you and me to give up our lives. He is the one who nourishes, heals, and protects us, providing guidance, and never takes anything from us without a reason. As Allah(ﷻ)asks in Surah Ar-Rahman, what favour will you and I deny from our Lord? How greatly He loves you and me! We do not need to have a switch to make our hearts beat, or be connected to an oxygen cylinder to breathe. We do not have to exert any effort for our brain to function, the brain which typically begins to suffer damage after about 3-4 minutes without oxygen. After 4-6 minutes irreversible brain damage is likely to occur and after 10 minutes, most brain functions could be lost leading to severe brain damage or brain death, our eyes to see in which the retina alone contains about 120 million rods (for low-light vision) and 6 million cones (for colour vision), or our ears to hear. Subhan Allah, He created us and gave us everything we need to live our lives in a way that pleases Him.

Did you know that each adult human body is estimated to have more than 46 miles of nerves and over 60,000 miles of blood vessels? Or that the brain alone has approximately 100 billion nerve cells? Or that just one foot is made up of 38 bones, 30 joints and more than 100 muscles, tendons, and ligaments which all have to work in unison just to allow us to walk?

What you and I will deny my dear sisters and brothers, what will we deny?

Love is when God says to you, "I have created everything for you."
And you say, "I have left everything for you"

– Rumi

What are you and I ready to leave? Not our life, at least patience to what we face? Can we?

Remembering Allah's plan and seeking His guidance, patience, and inner strength. Realising the pure love of Allah (ﷻ) leads us to remembering Him in every moment.

Ibn Al-Qayim (may Allah (ﷻ) have mercy on him) says: "Giving preference to the satisfaction of Allah, the Exalted and Glorious, over the satisfaction of anyone else means to want and to do whatever brings His satisfaction even if it dissatisfies the creatures.

What often leads us to experience emotional pain is our expectations. While it is natural to expect a fruitful relationship, it is important to understand that not all of our expectations may be met. Rather than dwelling on unmet expectations, it is better to put in your best efforts, play your role to the fullest, and then leave the rest in God's hands. If people do not honour or respect you, you need not worry or become depressed. Instead, focus on what is within your control and let go of what is not.

You have already been honoured by your Creator. Why then do you seek the honour and respect of His creations?

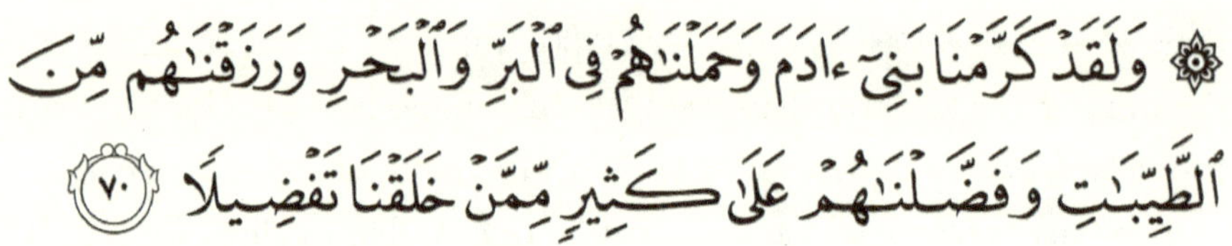

And We have certainly honoured the children of Adam and carried them on the land and sea and provided for them of the good things and preferred them over much of what We have created, with [definite] preference. Sahih International Quran 17:70

When we realise the true meaning of the struggles, we can understand that everything we go through has a purpose. Once, a doctor in an interview said, "I was a busy ortho specialist. Patients would wait a long time to see me, and they were happy with me. Most of them would complain to me, 'Doctor, we have pain,' and I used to joke, 'Small pain, right? Not big.' I didn't even know what they were going through until one day I met with an accident that sent me to the ICU, required operations, and had me bedridden in the hospital for months. At the hospital where I was working before, I realised I didn't see so many details of the treatments, even though I was a doctor. I went through all these experiences, which made me realise one thing: what is pain? Now I know what pain is, and I can say I treat my patients with empathy, seeing myself in them. Subhan Allah, you see the difference between seeing it and experiencing it.

Recently I went through the amazing book of Dr. Paul Brand -Pain The Gift nobody wants. Dr. Brand describes pain as essential to our survival. In his work with leprosy patients, he saw how the inability to feel pain led to severe injuries and infections because patients didn't realize they were hurt. Pain, he argues, is a built-in alarm system, alerting us to physical harm and forcing us to stop and care for ourselves.

Let's relate this to our life. As a mother, I was thinking when my little one started walking and was very curious about exploring everything she saw passing by. I still remember when she saw a lit candle. She always loved to try to catch it. No matter how much I tried to take her away from it, she always attempted to touch the yellow flame. Of course, she didn't know that it could hurt her until one day she felt the heat. If we couldn't feel heat or pain, a fire that could burn you wouldn't be dangerous, just a pretty flame to play with, wouldn't it?

A mother, accompanied by her 4-year-old child, visited Dr. Paul Brand. Her legs were infected and bandaged. Dr. Paul describes attempting to remove the bandages, revealing a leg covered in pus and blood, but the child surprisingly stayed calm. According to the mother, she never experiences pain. At the age of 2, she witnessed her biting her fingers and drawing with her own blood. I was thinking For the child, her fingers must have been like an ink pot filled with red ink, which she bit as if opening up the inkpot to take the paint and draw and color with it. Can you imagine the danger of not feeling pain? This is when I really said Alhamdulillah for the pain, my Rabb.

I vividly remember an option given to me by my gynecologist during my delivery. When I was pregnant with my elder daughter, I had to go through complete bed rest. I was literally instructed not to move. I felt like I was always holding a baby that could drop anytime. Having had miscarriages before, this baby was like a gem to us. My parents and husband were around the clock to watch how I moved, how I turned on the bed. It was nice to experience those days with utmost care and affection. Alhamdulillah for those days and pains I had to go through that makes my elder one so special. I was taken care of as much as possible to stretch my days without getting early delivery cramps, which was a goal set for me by my doctor because there were higher chances of premature delivery. Finally, when I ended up on the 24th week with cramps at the hospital, my doctor suggested getting admitted and returning home after delivery. After a month in the hospital bed with daily monitoring and injections, my doctor finally said, "I think the baby is healthy enough to go home now." Let's prepare for labor tomorrow." I got prepared after the long days finally; I was taken to the labor room to give the injections to induce labor pain. Before that, my doctor said, "There is an option for you, young lady. You can opt for a painless delivery. We can give you an injection, and you will have a good sleep at the time of the baby's arrival; you will just feel but no pain." Since it's my first baby and I was going through lots of pain and struggles during the last few months, I was like, shall I opt for it? But I saw two hands waving back of my doctor signaling to say no. My nurse, Sister Maryamma, she was a senior nurse, rather than a nurse; she has turned to me like my mother with affection from the last month, daily visits, daily routine checking my vitals, taking me for rounds. I said no, doctor, I'm ready to bear the pain. I didn't have any idea of the severity of the pain of introducing a new life to the world. The next few hours of pain, and literally, once I had to ask my doctor to please opt for a C-section to just get over the pain. I really remember those words of Sister Maryamma. She said, "You have to know the pain of bringing this life into the world so that you have an affection with your child. Unless you know that, you are just a robot with no feelings. If God willed, He could have allowed the birth without pain, but if He has intended the birth of a child to go through intense pain, then there is wisdom behind it." She continued, "Each time you are getting a hike of pain, remember you are going to see one of the wonderful smiles at the end, and all your pain will vanish in few minutes. Beautiful things don't happen without any pain." Those words gave me strength for the next hours, and after 15 hours of labor pain,

Allah (SWT)[1] blessed me with that little princess with sparkling eyes and a wonderful smile. As Sister Maryamma said, all the pain vanished in few minutes. Alhamdulillah

Similarly, if you look at charities, palliative centres, and other organisations serving humanity, you'll often find that the people behind them have experienced deep pain and loss. Isn't it amazing how pain can sometimes be a blessing in disguise, inspiring us to make a positive impact on the world? I'm excited to learn about the souls that I'll be sharing in your upcoming pages - those who have turned their pain into power to inspire others.

No pain, no gain, right?

As believers, we can certainly relate to the example provided. During the fasting of Ramadan, we crave a variety of foods, but upon breaking the fast, the most delicious drink is water.

The water becomes far more delicious than ever before after the long hours of thirst. Doesn't this thirst make us realise how delicious and blessed water truly is, something we may have taken for granted in the past?

Think of the air we breathe, the water we drink, the sunlight that warms our skin, the food that nourishes our bodies. These are all blessings from Allah that we often take for granted. But when we pause to appreciate them, a sense of awe and gratitude washes over us, reminding us of the abundance that surrounds us.

This awareness of blessings can extend to even the smallest details. The beauty of a flower, the song of a bird, the kindness of a stranger – these are all blessings that can enrich our lives if we open our hearts to receive them. Gratitude teaches us to appreciate the simple things, the

[1] SWT – Subhanahu wa ta'ala

ordinary moments that often go unnoticed, and to find beauty in the everyday.

And when we encounter challenges, moments of hardship, or even trials, gratitude becomes our anchor, our source of strength. It reminds us that even in the midst of darkness, Allah's blessings continue to flow, guiding us through the storm. It reminds us that our hardships are not the end of the story but rather opportunities for growth, refinement, and ultimately, greater blessings.

As per Robert A. Emmons in his famous book "The Psychology of Gratitude," he states as below,

> *All three components of gratitude resonate together in the French expression Je suis reconnaissant (I am grateful)—I recognize (intellectually), I acknowledge (willingly), I appreciate (emotionally). Only when all three come together is gratitude complete.*

Giving Thanks for abundance
Is sweeter than the abundance itself:
Should one who is absorbed with the Generous one
Be distracted by the gift?
Thankfulness is the soul of beneficence
Abundance is but the husk,
For thankfulness brings you to the place where the Beloved lives.
Abundance yeilds heedlessness;
Thankfulness brings alertness:
Hunt for bounty with the net of gratitude

– Rumi….

Mathnawi III 2879-2895
(Translated by Kabir Helminski and Camille Helminski)
The Rumi Collection

Chapter 3

Nurtured Souls

* * *

Do you know why, O faithful ones?
Listen to the truth the wise reveal-
Often in the desert, water is unseen,
But for the traveler, sand abounds.

– Rumi

Ali Bannat, an Australian Muslim businessman, aged 29, enjoyed life to the fullest, making the most of what the world had to offer. Ali received a devastating prognosis from the doctor, giving him only six months to live. He was diagnosed with cancer that had spread throughout his body. At this critical juncture, I urge my readers to put themselves in Ali's shoes. Imagine having to leave behind all the luxuries you have accumulated – the cars, mansions, designer clothes, and branded shoes – and facing a mere six months to live. Can you fathom it? In such a situation, one had a choice to make: either indulge in every desire for the remaining time or strive to lead a meaningful life. Ali chose the latter path.

A Muslim brother's funeral due to cancer made Ali realise he needed to prepare for the Hereafter, which he envisioned as beautiful. He knew he had to work in this world to gain Allah's love and pleasure and be successful in the Afterlife. So Ali decided to use his remaining time wisely. He sold all his possessions and travelled to Togo, embarking on a journey to establish a charitable organisation called MATW (Muslim Around the World)

Yes, Ali, you were right. Indeed, cancer was a gift for you. Otherwise, you would have remained a businessman wandering in the luxuries of the world. Now, as I sit in a corner of my home writing about you, someone in another part of the world is reading about you. Wasn't it a fact that Allah (ﷻ) had chosen you for a mission, and you have accomplished it? I make my sincere dua, may Allah (ﷻ) grant you Jannatul Firdaws, and may Allah (ﷻ) grant us the opportunity to be in His Jannah.

Ali lived for 3 years after being diagnosed with the deadly disease. In one of his interviews, he expressed gratitude, saying, "At this point in my life, Allah (ﷻ) has gifted me with cancer throughout my body. I have changed my whole life to helping people. I consider this a blessing, as Allah (ﷻ) has given me a chance to change. It has opened my eyes to every gift in my life, even the simple joy of breathing fresh air, which I had taken for granted before." He also acknowledged his blessings during the hardest moments of his illness, stating, "The greatest gift is the ability to wake up and be able to do our basic needs independently. We do this effortlessly each day, yet fail to appreciate it. Are we truly grateful for these everyday favours that we enjoy without any exertion on our part? Alhamdulillah, O Lord, we are indeed ungrateful. Please forgive us."

Despite the difficulties posed by his illness, Ali dedicated much of his time to to Africa. Even when he faced challenges like the tumour in his mouth that caused him to bleed, he remained focused on his mission - to build his akhirah (life in the afterlife) and serve as a reminder for others. He invested in agricultural tools to help people earn a living and escape poverty, as well as built mosques, schools, and water wells to improve their quality of life. Ali tirelessly worked to feed and support orphans and widows, leaving behind a legacy that has impacted millions. He has become an inspiration to those blessed with good health, wealth, and time.

He was busy feeding the orphans and supporting them and widows. He was setting a legacy ahead for millions to follow, an inspiration to those with health, wealth, and time. A legacy that has fed more than 90 million people.

Ali's passing in Ramadan marked the end of a remarkable journey.

He transformed from a businessman to a philanthropist, leaving a legacy that continues to inspire others.

Ali received a timely reminder and refocused his life on the right mission. Are we truly grateful to our Lord for the countless blessings He bestows upon us, or do we instead complain about what we lack? It is time to reflect deeply and renew our gratitude. If not now, then when?

Illuminating Souls from the Battlefield

Will you be able to watch your child suffer from trauma?
Will you be able to see your child suffering from hunger?
Your child lacking good education and clothing.
How anxious do we get when their school bus is late?
How much we worry about our little ones. Oh, my small one is having an exam, I am worried about her marks.

Fathima Bint Ismail

Oh no, her hair is falling. I think she is having a vitamin deficiency.

We often forget to take care of ourselves because we are focused on children, don't we? We often say, "My children are my life."

Then, what about those mothers and fathers who hold their little ones, who were once shining like a moon and the light of their lives, now lifeless in their arms... And they still say "Alhamdulillah."

What kind of resilience is this? From the battlefield to the world, a powerful message of resilience and faith without corruption. Seeing several videos and articles, I asked myself: am I a true servant of my Lord? Do I thank Him? Do I love Him as they did?

A Palestinian mother who lost her two young children mourns them in a beautiful poem. She says, "How lucky I was to have had you so beautifully, so fully. I questioned myself, what stroke of luck having you was, which filled me with so much love and gratitude. My beautiful gifts were returned to their creator."

Hanaa Abu Jabal, a 55-year-old mother of eight, shared her pain of losing a child in the war. "Losing a child for a mother means losing her soul... Imagine children dying in front of their parents due to malnutrition and hunger, yet the parents still say Alhamdulillah (praise be to God). Where do signs of love and blessings from their Lord, despite their hardships.

I can't forget the video of a businessman who lost everything in a war, including his life savings, in just a few hours. Despite this, he was found smiling and at peace. When asked why, he said, "

All that I had was given by my Lord; it was never mine. If Allah (ﷻ) has decided to take it back, it's his right and wisdom to do it. I love Him, so I don't get upset over these losses." He accepted the loss with love and gratitude, knowing that everything happens for a reason.

His resilience comes from a deep faith and trust in God. We often panic over delayed salaries, extra expenses, or losses, but where is our gratitude and trust in Allah? These events are a reminder for us to reflect, be grateful, and trust in Him. If not now, then when?

Young Soul of Determination

A few months ago, I was going through one of the most difficult tests in my life. I felt like I was on the edge of my patience and composure. I felt like I was losing control of my mind. My heart was racing most of the time. I couldn't eat or drink due to the emotional pain I was experiencing. Even pleasant nights seemed to be longer ones without sleep. I was physically and mentally drained. I often prayed to Allah, the Almighty, to give me the strength to face this challenge and to be able to keep complete trust in Him. I knew the phase was not easy, but as a believer, I had to shift my focus, which was a clear realisation for me.

After that phase, I am now here, writing this book, hoping it could help at least one soul in this world. What motivated me to write this book was my own pain. As a busy working mom, I had set aside many of my dreams and goals, focusing on my family. Taking care of your family is an act of worship, but being unique, finding your inner soul, your real purpose is very important as well. You as a creation of Allah (ﷻ) have a unique purpose; we came alone and we will return alone, and that's a fact. Now, how are we preparing for it?

You and I need to build our own identities. A clear realisation for each of us is crucial. I came across the inspiring life of a young soul who was in her teens.

She was a smart, energetic young girl, excelling in her studies and as a national basketball player, loved by everyone. She had to face a great tragedy in her life. An hour of that beautiful dawn turned out to be one of the most terrifying moments in her life. She fell down from the terrace of her hostel, slipping on the rainwater. After waking up in the hospital bed, following hours of sedation, she realised she could no longer walk. Her spinal cord injury left her paraplegic (Paraplegia is a form of paralysis that mostly affects the movement of the lower body). She had to undergo continuous surgeries and treatments. Doctors told her she would be bedridden forever.

There are a number of inspiring stories in the world, but what made me so affected by this young soul was that she was the age of my daughter. I was seeing my daughter's face in her. What made me have a second thought was her statement. "I was crying for two months continuously, I was mentally down. I needed to continue my studies but my thought was how I would go in a wheelchair to school. A person who dreamed of being the best basketball player is now in a wheelchair. In some moments, I thought there was no point in living like this. Many of those who I thought would be beside me left me when I was in my wheelchair. I had only my mom who was supportive as I lost my father in my childhood. My first step was to accept my situation. I was a person who always believed in God. I knew if God had placed me in this situation, I had something to do further. There were two choices in front of me. One was I could remain as I am, crying and complaining about my situation. The second one was 'Happened is Happened, now what's next? How can I come back? What's my next role to be played in my life?' I chose the second one, and that changed my life.

"I realised I need to live independently and find ways to thrive in a wheelchair. After much research, I discovered the possibilities of para-sports. The first step was to courageously face people."

Then, her journey of courage and resilience began, as she placed her complete trust in God. She understood that God had a purpose for her in this situation. Within just two years, this remarkable woman, Ms. Alphia James, became the world's number 10 para badminton player. The lesson I learned from her was the importance of trust in God, gratitude, acceptance, hard work, clear goals, and determination. She was a true embodiment of resilience and her journey of resilience continues aiming for the Olympic medal ahead.

I from my heart wish all the best and may God bless you to achieve all your goals, little soul. May your journey inspire generations to come. Don't get depressed with small failures in life.

After I went through her story of struggles, I looked at myself. I said, "My Lord, forgive me. My hands and legs are fine, I'm walking without pain, I'm breathing without difficulty, I don't have to put any effort to make sure my organs are working. I can swallow my food easily. I have lots of blessings. Why am I drained and depressed? It's time to change… Time of realisation comes through pain, so if so, that pain was also a blessing, right?"

Looking at my own life, I found that self-reflection is crucial. We are often quick to find fault in others, but forget to look inward. When I started my journey with the Qur'an, the first thing I needed to change was myself. Seeking the right knowledge is important to discern right from wrong.

It's like our physical health - we eagerly get routine check-ups and take precautions when the doctor diagnoses an issue, like diabetes. We change our diets and fight our cravings to ensure our physical well-being. But what about the health of our soul, our inner self? Shouldn't we also do regular "check-ups" and make necessary changes there? After all, our inner health is what truly reflects outwardly.

I was short-tempered, and it was only when I embarked on my Quranic journey that I realised this was the first thing I needed to work on.

The busyness of life was no excuse - it was something I had to overcome. There are moments when I want to react angrily, but I have to struggle to contain my emotions. It is important for me to avoid saying anything that would upset my Lord. My goal has shifted from pleasing people to pleasing my Creator, who gave me life, nourished me, healed me, and never forsakes me.

Fathima Bint Ismail

Chapter 4

Hunger – The Aching Deaths

* * *

Income Multiplies from giving and spending -
So that Muhammad, the king of prosperity, has said,
"O possessors of wealth, generosity is a gainful trade."
Riches were never lessened by sharing:
In truth, acts of charity increase ones's wealth.

– *Rumi*

Scripting out the words for my book while having a cup of brewed coffee on my table, sipping it in between my writing, makes me feel more refreshed. Alhamdulillah for the cup of coffee. Now, let me take you on a journey of food. Isn't everyone excited? I believe one of the most interesting topics, or rather a display of luxury in life nowadays, is experiencing different types of food. Let me take you to my kitchen at the moment. I have delicious chicken gravy and ghee rice today. For my little ones, I have prepared fruit salad as well. Since it's the weekend, I have some extra time to cook them better dishes. Now I would like to take you to your kitchen, can you have a look at the foods in your kitchen or your fridges?

You may not have cooked food right now, but you have the option to order and have food delivered.

We are often so accustomed to the abundance of food, water, and air that we take these blessings for granted. We wake up each morning, open our refrigerators, and find plenty of choices – fresh fruits, vegetables, grains, and meats – readily available. We turn on the tap and clean water flows effortlessly, quenching our thirst. We inhale deeply, filling our lungs with the life-giving oxygen of the atmosphere, without a second thought. These are the simple, essential elements of life, yet they are so often overlooked in the rush of our daily routines.

Imagine for a moment what it would be like to live without these necessities. Picture yourself parched, your throat dry and cracked, with no source of fresh water in sight. Imagine the gnawing hunger that consumes you, the emptiness in your stomach that no amount of willpower can quell. Now, imagine the suffocating sensation of being deprived of air, the desperate struggle to breathe. These are the stark realities that millions of people around the world face every single day.

Do we thank our Lord for the abundance of food options on our tables today? What about throughout the entire years? Personally, I have to admit that I have not been as grateful as I should be. I apologise if this topic may be repetitive, but I cannot ignore it as my book will be incomplete without this topic.

Gratitude is not a one-time event; it is an ongoing journey. By cultivating a heart filled with gratitude, we can transform our lives, bringing more joy, peace, and fulfilment. As we recognise and appreciate the blessings we have received, we open ourselves up to receiving even more. And most importantly, we live a life that honours the generosity of Allah, the Giver of all good things.

My father was very strict about us finishing our food on our plates. He never liked to see food or water being wasted. He had a habit of always making sure the pipes were closed so that water wouldn't be wasted. Perhaps because I saw him doing this from a young age, I also developed the blessed quality of not wasting water. I feel guilty when I see water being wasted. Alhamdulillah, when I got married, my husband also values these qualities and he makes sure neither me nor our kids waste any food or water. He shares his childhood struggles of not having enough food, and I am grateful for the experiences that shaped him. Perhaps if he hadn't faced those challenges, he may not have developed this quality.

Do you know what's the biggest blessing we could have? It's food, clean water, the oxygen we breathe, the ability to have it without struggling. When I am writing about the food and water repetitively, do you know how many children and adults are dying at this moment due to hunger?

According to the United Nations Food and Agriculture Organization (FAO), estimates that over 820 million people worldwide are facing chronic hunger, meaning they don't get enough food to live an active, healthy life. This translates to one in ten people globally struggling to access enough food for their basic needs. The majority of these individuals reside in developing countries, where poverty, conflict, and climate change exacerbate the situation.

If we visit Worldometers.info, we can find real-time statistics on key factors like birth rate, death rate, and more. At the moment I am writing this, the number of people who have died of hunger today is 21,410, and this number continues to increase every minute. The statistics are staggering, but they only begin to tell the story. Behind every number, there is a human face, a family struggling to survive, a child whose future hangs in the balance.

Let's reflect on hunger. As devout Muslims, we feel hungry while fasting in the sacred month of Ramadan. We all experience hunger and thirst for a short period of time, eagerly anticipating breaking our fast in the evening with various foods. While we know we will have what we desire at the end of the day when we feel hungry, what about those who have no hope of ever eating? Can you imagine dying from hunger, how many hours and days without food it takes for a person's life to be lost?

As per NPR research on starvation:

A severe lack of food for a prolonged period—not enough calories of any sort to keep up with the body's energy needs—is starvation. The body's reserve resources are depleted. The result is substantial weight loss, wasting away of the body's tissues, and eventually death.

When faced with starvation, the body fights back. The first day without food is a lot like the overnight fast between dinner one night and breakfast the next morning. Energy levels are low but pick up with a morning meal.

Within days, faced with nothing to eat, the body begins feeding on itself. "The body starts to consume energy stores — carbohydrates, fats and then the protein parts of tissue," says Maureen Gallagher, senior nutrition adviser to Action Against Hunger, a network of international humanitarian organisations focused on eliminating hunger. Metabolism slows, the body cannot regulate its temperature, kidney function is impaired, and the immune system weakens.

When the body uses its reserves to provide basic energy needs, it can no longer supply necessary nutrients to vital organs and tissues. The heart, lungs, ovaries, and testes shrink. Muscles shrink, and people feel weak. Body temperature drops, and people can feel chilled. People can become irritable, and it becomes difficult to concentrate.

Eventually, nothing is left for the body to scavenge except muscle. "Once protein stores start getting used, death is not far," says Dr. Nancy Zucker, director of the Duke Center for Eating Disorders at Duke University. "You're consuming your own muscle, including the heart muscle." In the late stages of starvation, people can experience hallucinations, convulsions, and disruptions in heart rhythm. Finally, the heart stops.

The body attempts to protect the brain, says Zucker, by shutting down the most metabolically intense functions first, like digestion, resulting in diarrhoea. "The brain is relatively protected, but eventually we worry about neuronal death and brain matter loss," she says. Just as the heart, lungs, and other organs weaken and shrivel without food, eventually so does the brain.

"It's hard to know. Children suffer more steeply, but their recovery might be better. It might be a tie," says Zucker. "But adults and children alike can have permanent brain damage."

How long does this take? There's great variation in the amount of time people can survive without food, depending on age, body weight, whether they have adequate water, and whether they have other underlying health issues.

For some it's 21 days, for some it's a few months, but can you imagine the agony of death due to hunger? We, as humans, take everything for granted: the food we have, the clean water, clothes, jobs, relationships. However, we must acknowledge that these are not obtained through our own efforts; they are the most amazing blessings we could ever receive.

The most intriguing aspect of attending my Quran class was contemplating on every Ayah. I recall a week when the lessons centred on the importance of food and water. I visited the market to purchase fish and groceries. I was brought to tears by the variety of fish on display. I stopped briefly to ponder, "Oh Allah, how great is your love for us." You could have chosen to create just one kind of fish, but instead, you opted to make multiple kinds with varied flavours. There are individuals who enjoy seafood, while others do not. Some people have a preference for large fish, whereas others enjoy catching smaller ones. Some people like prawns, while others favour crabs. Have we ever pondered the reason behind our Lord's creation of such diversity? Could he have created only one kind, and we would have been satisfied, correct?

Similarly,

He could have created only one type of fruit, but why the varieties? Why the different types of vegetables? Have we ever pondered over this? No, because we often take everything for granted. I used to be the same, but when I started thinking and reflecting, I could taste the pure love and care of my Lord.

If we take some time in a day to just look around us, the nature, the sunlight that brings energy to us, the moon charming in the night, and the beautiful sky decorated with twinkling stars, the rain that falls from the sky, the trees around us. I could go on and on writing, but as Allah (ﷻ), The Exalted says.

وَلَوْ أَنَّمَا فِي ٱلْأَرْضِ مِن شَجَرَةٍ أَقْلَٰمٌ وَٱلْبَحْرُ يَمُدُّهُۥ مِنۢ بَعْدِهِۦ
سَبْعَةُ أَبْحُرٍ مَّا نَفِدَتْ كَلِمَٰتُ ٱللَّهِ ۗ إِنَّ ٱللَّهَ عَزِيزٌ حَكِيمٌ ﴿٢٧﴾

Sahih International
And if whatever trees upon the earth were pens and the sea [was ink], replenished thereafter by seven [more] seas, the words of Allah (ﷻ), The Exalted would not be exhausted. Indeed, Allah (ﷻ), The Exalted is Exalted in Might and Wise. 31:27

The Qur'an reminds us that lies in the fact that we are surrounded by an abundance of blessings, yet we often fail to recognise them. From the air we breathe to the food we consume, from the warmth of the sun to the beauty of the natural world, countless blessings are bestowed upon us daily, yet we often take them for granted.

We will delve into the concept of justice, the power of community, and the pursuit of peace, all of which are interconnected to the journey of finding fulfilment and leaving a positive mark on the world.

He Prophet Muhammad (peace be upon him) said, "The best of you are those who are most beneficial to others." This profound statement speaks to the essence of a fulfilled life. The true measure of abundance is not measured by material possessions, but by the impact we make on the lives of others. It is in sharing our blessings, in alleviating the richness of life.

This is not to say that material wealth is inherently bad. The Qur'an acknowledges that wealth and possessions are part of Allah's creation and can be a source of blessing if used wisely and with a conscious intention to benefit others. The key lies in our attitude towards these blessings. Are we grateful for what we have, or are we consumed by a relentless pursuit of more?

The Quran reminds us of our responsibility to care for the poor and needy.

As we reflect on the shadows of hunger and poverty, we must recognise our responsibility to the world. The suffering of others affects us all, reminding us of our shared humanity and the imperative to act with compassion and empathy. The Qur'an teaches us that helping the needy is not merely an act of charity but a profound act of worship, drawing us closer to Allah (ﷻ) and reminding us of the blessings we often take for granted.

Let our hearts be filled with compassion, our hands extended in service, and our voices raised in advocacy, echoing the message of the Quran:

> *"And spend in the way of Allah, and do not throw yourselves into destruction with your own hands." (Quran, 2:195)*

In the coming chapters, we will explore the practical ways to cultivate gratitude, the importance of compassion and service in addressing global suffering, and the role of faith and spirituality in guiding us on a path of purpose and meaning.

Chapter 5

The Gem – Gems of Generosity

* * *

"If you become a helper of hearts, springs of wisdom will flow from your heart."

–Jalal ad-Din Rumi

Be that unique soul - who feels the pain of others, who feels the hunger of others. We are on a journey of treasure hunt, right? I can't pass by without this. How many years will we live here? I cannot ignore this. How long will we reside here? Perhaps when you read my book, I may no longer be alive, but I am composing it as a part of my mission - my mission, calling you all towards goodness. I hope my words reach you. I hope my words touch you, inspire you. Yes, while you may have read countless similar topics before, I truly believe that any words spoken from the heart with genuine intention make a huge impact on at least one soul.

A Beacon of Hope for the Needy

Imagine a world where hunger and poverty are a pandemic, where families struggle to put food on the table, and children go to bed with empty stomachs. This grim reality is the daily struggle for millions around the globe. Charity acts as a lifeline, a beacon of hope in the midst of despair.

A simple act of giving, whether it be a meal, a warm blanket, or financial assistance, can make a world of difference to those in need. It can alleviate immediate suffering, provide basic necessities, and empower individuals to rebuild their lives. By providing financial support, we enable individuals to break free from the shackles of poverty, allowing them to access education, healthcare, and opportunities for economic self-sufficiency.

The Prophet Muhammad (peace be upon him) said, "The best of deeds are those that benefit others." This profound statement speaks to the inherent goodness and righteousness of helping others. When we alleviate suffering, we not only uplift the lives of those in need but also fulfil a fundamental obligation of our faith.

The Power of Intention

The intention behind giving is crucial. When we give out of pure love for Allah, seeking His pleasure and desiring to help others in need, our act of charity becomes a powerful form of worship. It elevates our actions from mere generosity to acts of sincere devotion.

The Prophet Muhammad (peace be upon him) said, "Indeed, every good deed is charity." This profound statement underscores the importance of intention in our actions.

In practical terms, acts of kindness can take many forms. It could be as simple as offering a smile to a stranger, helping an elderly person carry groceries, or volunteering at a local food bank. These seemingly insignificant gestures, when multiplied across a community, have the potential to create a ripple effect of compassion and kindness that extends far beyond the initial act.

The impact of kindness goes far beyond addressing immediate needs. It has the power to heal emotional wounds, rebuild broken relationships, and inspire hope in those who have lost their way.

Therefore, let us strive to live our lives guided by the principles of compassion, empathy, and kindness. Let us reach out to those in need, not only with material aid, but also with a generous spirit and a heart that overflows with love and understanding. For in the act of giving, we receive something far more precious – a sense of purpose, a connection to the divine, and a legacy of compassion that will extend far beyond our lifetime.

This path of service is not about seeking recognition or personal gain. It's about embracing the opportunity to extend a hand of kindness, to share our blessings with those in need. It's about recognising that every act of service, no matter how small, has the potential to ripple outward, creating positive change in the lives of others and leaving a lasting impact on the world.

Imagine the profound joy of bringing a smile to a child's face by donating to an orphanage, the sense of peace that comes with volunteering at a local soup kitchen, or the deep satisfaction of offering a helping hand to a neighbour in need. These actions, seemingly ordinary in themselves, hold the power to transform both the giver and the receiver, fostering a spirit of compassion, empathy, and unity within our communities.

This journey of service is not without its challenges. It requires us to step out of our comfort zones, to confront our own biases and prejudices, and to open our hearts to those who may be different from us. Yet, it is precisely in these moments of selflessness that we discover the true meaning of our existence, the profound connection we share with humanity, and the infinite blessings that come with living a life dedicated to making a positive difference.

The Qur'an urges us to reflect upon the plight of those less fortunate, to consider the hunger and thirst they endure. This reflection is not merely an intellectual exercise. It's a call to action, a reminder of our responsibility to alleviate suffering and to contribute to the betterment of the world.

Let us embark on this journey of service with open hearts, embracing the countless opportunities that surround us. Let us recognise that even the smallest act of kindness, the simplest gesture of compassion, can have a profound impact.

Let us strive to embody the spirit of service, not only as a means of finding purpose in our lives but also as a way of honouring the divine calling we have been given. For in serving others, we are truly serving Allah (ﷻ) and fulfilling the essence of our existence.

Small Acts, Big Impact:

Let us begin with the seemingly insignificant, for it is in these small acts that profound change can take root. A smile offered to a stranger, a kind word spoken to a neighbour, a helping hand extended to someone in need – these seemingly simple gestures have the power to break down barriers and build bridges of connection.

Your one decision, your one hand towards the needy, your words of compassion and kindness can make changes to lives.

The choice is yours... Be that unique one among the millions.
Be that enchanting flower chosen to be part of the bouquet.
From numerous petals of flowers, yours might be the one to touch the heart.
Your one decision can be the ripple that turns into a wave.

"In compassion and grace, be like the sun...
In concealing other's faults, be like the night...
In generosity and helping others, be like a river...
In anger and fury, be like dead...
In modesty and humility, be like the earth...
In tolerance, be like the sea...
Either appear as you are, or be as you appear.."

– Rumi

Chapter 6

Pandemic Blessings: A Spiritual Perspective

* * *

The Covid-19 pandemic, the world held its breath. A whisper of a new virus originating in a distant land quickly escalated into a global health crisis.

The invisible enemy, a microscopic entity with an unparalleled power to disrupt life, began to spread its tentacles, reaching every corner of the globe.

Initially, the outbreak was met with confusion and denial. The complete magnitude of the threat was hard to comprehend, and many dismissed it as a mere flu, a fleeting inconvenience. But as cases surged and the death toll mounted, the gravity of the situation became undeniably clear. **The world was in a state of emergency.**

Lockdowns became the new normal, as streets emptied, businesses shuttered, and the once bustling cities stood eerily silent. An era of social distancing, forcing individuals to isolate themselves from loved ones, a painful sacrifice made for the greater good. The once-familiar rhythm of life was disrupted, as routines were shattered and replaced with an uncertain future. Anxiety, fear, and uncertainty gnawed at the hearts and minds of individuals, creating a sense of unease that penetrated every aspect of life.

A Humbling Reminder

The pandemic's arrival, like thunder, shattered the rhythm of our lives. The world, once teeming with activity, fell into an eerie silence, a testament to the potent force that had taken hold. Cities, once vibrant with life, were eerily deserted, their streets echoing with an unfamiliar quiet. The once-crowded streets, now empty and deserted.

The pandemic's grip extended far beyond the confines of our homes, reaching into the very heart of our existence, forcing us to confront the fragility of our own existence.

It was in this unprecedented moment of global turmoil that we were confronted with our own weakness. We were reminded, in no uncertain terms, that we are not invincible, that our power is limited, and that our lives are ultimately in the hands of a higher power. The pandemic, in its unforgiving sweep, exposed the illusion of our control. We were stripped bare, stripped of our sense of security and our reliance on our own abilities, left to grapple with the stark reality of our dependence on the divine.

The pandemic's humbling effect was profound. It forced us to acknowledge our inherent vulnerability, to relinquish our illusion of control, and to seek solace in the divine. We were reminded that true power resides not in our own hands but in the hands of the Divine. The pandemic became a potent reminder that we are but mere mortals, entrusted with a temporary gift, a life to live, a journey to undertake, and a purpose to fulfil.

In the face of such immense power, it was impossible to remain indifferent. The pandemic's relentless march, its relentless sweep across the globe, demanded a response. We were compelled to confront the fragility of our own existence, to acknowledge our dependence on the divine, and to seek solace in the strength that lies beyond our own. ***We were called upon to shed our pride, to let go of our ego, and to surrender to the will of the Creator.***

Primarily associated with significant losses. These losses encompass the loss of life, jobs, and wealth, prompting many families to relocate from overseas back to their home countries.

Working in a travel company, I have witnessed numerous families grappling with dire situations during this period, with their sole request being a flight ticket to return home. Many found themselves stranded without access to food, yet we witnessed a global outpouring of support and assistance.

The Hidden Blessings

The lockdown imposed by the pandemic, though initially a source of anxiety and disruption, presented a unique opportunity for self-assessment. It was a time of forced solitude, where the relentless pace of life abruptly ceased, allowing for a profound exploration of our inner selves. The world had been put on hold, and with it, our usual routines, obligations, and distractions. This unexpected pause provided a canvas upon which we could examine our priorities, our values, and the very meaning we attributed to our existence.

As we all remained confined to our rooms, each of us had unique experiences. While my encounter may not have been vastly different from others, I must admit that the Covid-19 pandemic, in my perspective, brought about some blessings. It provided an opportunity for introspection on how it positively impacted relationships.

One of the blessings I encountered was the initiation of my journey with the Quran. Previously, my search for classes to attend was hindered by the lack of online options, making it challenging as a working mother. However, the widespread availability of online classes during the pandemic facilitated my learning from the comfort of home, eliminating the need for travel. This period also allowed me to spend valuable time with my husband and children, fostering stronger bonds.

We were left with the bare necessities of life - food, shelter, and the company of our immediate family. The pandemic compelled us to adapt to a lifestyle with minimal resources, encouraging us to curtail unnecessary expenses and celebrations. We discovered that happiness didn't reside in material possessions or social acclaim, but in the simple joys of human connection, the beauty of nature, and the quiet moments of reflection.

The pandemic also prompted a deep reflection on our faith. The uncertainty of the future, the fear of the unknown, and the fragility of life ignited a spiritual awakening in many. The search for solace and meaning led individuals back to their faith, seeking guidance and strength from a higher power. The isolation, instead of diminishing our faith, served to strengthen it, as we sought solace and purpose in our connection to the Divine.

The pandemic, in its unwelcome arrival, inadvertently bestowed a precious gift: **a time** for reassessment and rediscovery. The unexpected stillness of the world allowed us to find our true selves, to appreciate the simple joys of life, and to reconnect with the deeper meaning that transcends the ephemeral nature of this world.

The echoes of nature's response reverberated across the globe. Factories closed, airplanes grounded, and bustling city streets transformed into eerie, silent landscapes. The air, once choked with exhaust fumes and particulate matter, began to clear.

On a global scale, studies by the National Institute of Health (NIH) revealed positive environmental impacts during the pandemic. Social movement restrictions led to improved air quality and reduced water contamination in various regions worldwide. The decrease in atmospheric pollution and greenhouse gas emissions was notable, attributed to reduced industrial and transportation activities during lockdown. The World Health Organization reported a significant decrease in air pollution in many urban areas, with some cities experiencing the cleanest air they had seen in decades.

In countries like China, significant reductions in greenhouse gas emissions and improved air quality were observed due to industrial and transportation shutdowns. The pandemic also resulted in decreased water pollution in developing countries like India, Pakistan, and Bangladesh, as industrial pollutants were minimised during the lockdown.

Furthermore, noise pollution levels decreased in major cities during the pandemic, offering relief from the adverse health effects associated with excessive noise. The pandemic served as a stark reminder of the vulnerability of even the most advanced medical technologies in the face of a minuscule virus, prompting valuable lessons and reflections.

Our lockdown was important for the nature to heal. The pandemic, in its unsettling truth, forced us to confront the delicate balance between humanity and nature. The planet's response, as a silent witness, was both a warning and an invitation.

Let's Reflect

The pandemic, with its abrupt halt to our accustomed routines, presented an unexpected opportunity—a chance to step back and reassess the things we held dear, to sift through the clutter of our lives and discern what truly mattered. It was a time when the relentless pursuit of material wealth and social status seemed to lose its lustre, replaced by a quiet longing for simplicity and connection. This period of enforced isolation became a catalyst for many to re-evaluate their priorities, to shed the layers of complexity that had come to define their lives, and to rediscover the profound joy that can be found in the essentials. We discovered that true happiness did not reside in material possessions or worldly achievements, but in the simple pleasures of life – a warm cup of tea, a phone call with a loved one, or a moment of quiet reflection.

We saw people dying due to a lack of oxygen. Oxygen cylinders ran short, and people were unable to breathe. Did we ever think of appreciating our Lord for giving us fresh air and the ability to breathe without difficulty?

COVID-19 instilled certain habits in us. For example, I'm pretty sure we are still in the habit of washing our hands, using sanitiser, and wearing masks when we are in a crowd. Hasn't it taught us good habits? It taught the world the steps to take if any pandemic or worse could strike the world, similar to how we do mock drills in school to be prepared, right? Similarly, it was another drill for us to be prepared.

The world of medical science and technology, which is at its peak compared to previous years, was actually shaken by a tiny speck of a virus. Can you imagine, a tiny virus that cannot be seen with the naked eye taught the world many lessons?

The pandemic highlighted the limitations of wealth in addressing essential needs, emphasising the importance of resilience and adaptability. It underscored the link between global health and the necessity for collective action in combating crises.

In conclusion, the Covid-19 pandemic, while fraught with challenges and losses, also presented opportunities for personal growth, environmental healing, and reflection. It serves as a reminder of the resilience and adaptability of humanity in the face of adversity, urging us to embrace positive changes and lessons learned during this unprecedented time.

Do you believe it was all a coincidence, without any reason behind it? Shift your perspective. Reflect deeply, and you will derive numerous lessons. Sometimes, God must guide you through lockdowns, knowing you will only develop certain habits by going through such experiences. Similarly, in our everyday lives, we may face small-scale "lockdowns." As mentioned, shift your thoughts, reflect, and renew. You possess an inner light; embrace it.

Discovering Hidden Talents and Passions

The unexpected pause brought by the pandemic, the job loss, the financial constraints, forced many a unique opportunity for self-discovery.

Many individuals, including housewives, ventured into online channels and home vegetable cultivation, promoting pesticide-free produce. Moreover, individuals who returned to their home countries from overseas employment initiated new businesses and startups, which have flourished.

The pandemic also prompted many individuals to explore new skills and interests. The constraints of confinement led to a desire for self-improvement, and people sought ways to fill the void created by the lack of social interaction. Online platforms became a haven for learning new languages, acquiring cooking skills, pursuing digital marketing, or mastering a musical instrument. The lockdown transformed homes into learning spaces, fostering a renewed curiosity and a drive to expand one's horizons.

Redefining Success

The pandemic, in its relentless march across the globe, disrupted not only our routines and social interactions, but also our deeply ingrained notions of success. The world we once knew, driven by the pursuit of material wealth, status, and fleeting pleasures, was suddenly thrown into disarray. As we faced the stark reality of our vulnerability, a profound shift in our values and priorities began to take place.

The pandemic's impact on our relationship with the world was profound and multifaceted. It forced us to re-evaluate our priorities, questioning the relentless pursuit of material gain and recognising the importance of connection, community, and living with intention.

As we navigate the post-pandemic world, it is imperative that we do not simply return to our pre-pandemic routines, but rather carry forward the lessons learned and strive to create a better future for ourselves and the world. The pandemic has exposed the vulnerabilities within our systems and challenged our fundamental assumptions about life, work, and our place in the cosmos. It has forced us to confront our priorities, re-evaluate our values, and reconnect with what truly matters.

Chapter 7

Nature Amazes Us – Reflections on Nature's Gifts

* * *

ٱللَّهُ ٱلَّذِى خَلَقَ ٱلسَّمَٰوَٰتِ وَٱلْأَرْضَ وَأَنزَلَ مِنَ ٱلسَّمَآءِ مَآءً
فَأَخْرَجَ بِهِۦ مِنَ ٱلثَّمَرَٰتِ رِزْقًا لَّكُمْ ۖ وَسَخَّرَ لَكُمُ ٱلْفُلْكَ
لِتَجْرِىَ فِى ٱلْبَحْرِ بِأَمْرِهِۦ ۖ وَسَخَّرَ لَكُمُ ٱلْأَنْهَٰرَ ﴿٣٢﴾

Sahih International
It is Allah (ﷻ), The Exalted who created the heavens and the earth and sent down rain from the sky and produced thereby some fruits as provision for you and subjected for you the ships to sail through the sea by His command and subjected for you the rivers.

Quran 14:32

وَسَخَّرَ لَكُمُ ٱلشَّمْسَ وَٱلْقَمَرَ دَآئِبَيْنِ ۖ وَسَخَّرَ لَكُمُ ٱلَّيْلَ
وَٱلنَّهَارَ ﴿٣٣﴾

Sahih International
And He subjected for you the sun and the moon, continuous [in orbit], and subjected for you the night and the day.

Quran 14:33

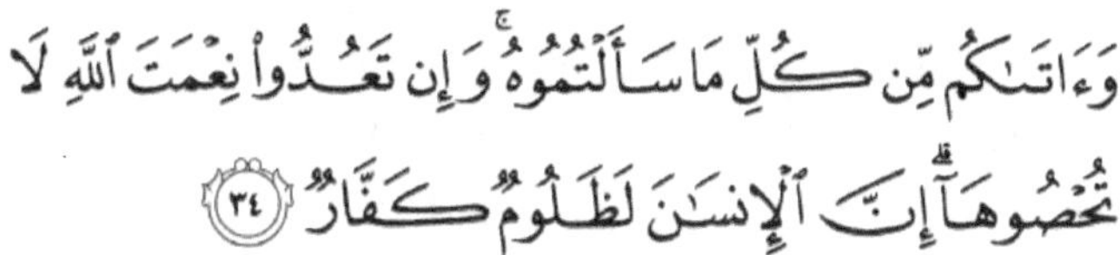

Sahih International
And He gave you from all you asked of Him. And if you should count the favor of Allah (ﷻ) you could not enumerate them. Indeed, mankind is [generally] most unjust and ungrateful.

Quran 14:34

When we are on the journey towards finding the treasure, one of the main steps is contemplating Allah's (ﷻ) creations. From the vastness of the cosmos to the microscopic world of cells, from the majestic mountains to the teeming oceans, our journey of reflection starts.

By observing the world around us with a mindful heart, we can gain deeper insight into His attributes, His purpose, and His boundless love for His creation. The Quran, the divine revelation to Prophet Muhammad (peace be upon him), is replete with verses that call upon us to reflect upon nature and recognise the signs of Allah's creation. "Indeed, in the creation of the heavens and the earth, and in the alternation of night and day, there are signs for people of understanding" (Quran 3:190).

These verses serve as a constant invitation to observe, contemplate, and appreciate the wonders that surround us.

My aim for this journey was modest, not intended to make you feel bored. Therefore, I have tried to present it as concisely as possible. However, without this topic, our journey would be akin to a road with no clear destination.

When I used to go through intense pain, I always felt peace when speaking with my Lord because I knew He was listening. Looking at the sky, seeing the shining stars and bright moon, I would feel a sense of happiness. Don't you find that too? Sitting alone, gazing up at the sky where I would whisper to my Lord, my words would become more beautiful. For me, that was one of the moments that brought peace to my heart. I believe one of the reasons Allah, the Exalted, adorned the sky with such beautiful stars and the moon was for us to experience this tranquillity.

The beauty of nature is a constant reminder of Allah's infinite artistry and perfect design. From the delicate petals of a flower to the vast expanse of the sky, each creation exhibits a captivating harmony and aesthetic appeal that speaks to the depths of Allah's creativity. The Quran, Allah's divine revelation, repeatedly highlights the beauty of creation, urging us to contemplate and reflect upon its wonders.

Imagine a single tree standing tall in a forest. Its roots burrow deep into the earth, drawing nourishment from the soil and water. Its leaves reach towards the sky, absorbing sunlight and releasing oxygen into the atmosphere. This tree, in its seemingly solitary existence, is intricately linked to its surroundings. The birds build nests in its branches, finding shelter and a place to raise their young. Squirrels scamper through its foliage, gathering nuts and seeds. Insects pollinate its flowers, ensuring the continuation of its species. The tree, in its quiet presence, provides sustenance and habitat for countless other creatures.

The interconnection of creation extends far beyond the boundaries of a single forest. The ocean, vast and mysterious, teems with life, providing food for millions of creatures, both on land and in the water. The delicate balance of the marine ecosystem is essential for the health of the planet as a whole. Whales, majestic giants of the deep, play a crucial role in regulating the ocean's carbon cycle, absorbing vast amounts of carbon dioxide from the atmosphere and storing it in their bodies. Their migration patterns help to distribute nutrients throughout the oceans, supporting the intricate food web that sustains countless other species.

The interconnection of all things is a profound reminder of the delicate balance and interdependence of life on Earth. The air we breathe, the water we drink, the food we eat – all are interconnected, forming a complex and interconnected web of life. Each element of creation, from the smallest microorganism to the largest planet, plays a vital role in sustaining this web.

The Quran, the divine revelation of Allah (ﷻ), emphasises the interconnection of all things, reminding us to observe and reflect upon the signs of His creation. The verses of the Quran speak of the delicate balance of nature, the interdependence of living beings, and the intricate web of relationships that connect everything in the universe. For example, in Surah Al-Anbiya, verse 30, Allah (ﷻ) states:

وَمِنْ ءَايَٰتِهِۦ خَلْقُ ٱلسَّمَٰوَٰتِ وَٱلْأَرْضِ وَمَا بَثَّ فِيهِمَا مِن دَآبَّةٍ ۚ وَهُوَ
عَلَىٰ جَمْعِهِمْ إِذَا يَشَآءُ قَدِيرٌ ﴿٢٩﴾

> ***"And among His signs is the creation of the heavens and the earth, and the living creatures that He has spread through them. And He is able to gather them together whenever He wills."***
>
> ***Quran 42:29***

This verse emphasises the unity and connection of all creation, from the heavens to the earth and all the creatures that inhabit them. Allah, the Creator, is able to bring all things together, demonstrating His absolute power and control over His creation. As humans, we are not separate from nature but part of it, intricately connected to the web of life. Our actions, whether positive or negative, have far-reaching consequences for the environment and for the well-being of all living beings.

The act of reflecting upon these wonders cultivates a sense of awe and humility within us. We are reminded of our own insignificance compared to the vastness of Allah's creation, and our hearts are filled with gratitude for His infinite blessings. This contemplation fosters a deeper connection to our Creator, nurturing our faith and strengthening our belief in His power and mercy. Observing and reflecting on the wonders of nature is a powerful act of worship that draws us closer to Allah. It fosters a deeper appreciation for His artistry, strengthens our faith, and cultivates a sense of awe and humility. By engaging in this practice, we not only connect with the Divine but also gain a greater understanding of the intricate balance of Allah's creation, reminding us of our responsibility as stewards of this precious world.

Imagine a world without milk. A world where the gentle, comforting warmth of a glass of milk on a cold day, the creamy sweetness of a milkshake, or the rich, cheesy goodness of a pizza are all but a distant memory. This might sound unimaginable, but it's a reality that many people around the world experience. The cow, with its remarkable ability to produce milk, stands as a testament to Allah's boundless mercy and provision. The cow, a creature of gentle nature and incredible biological design, embodies the essence of Allah's nurturing care. Its milk, a liquid gold brimming with essential nutrients, is a gift bestowed upon humanity, nourishing generations and sustaining lives. This remarkable liquid, produced by the cow's udder, is a symphony of complex biological processes, a masterpiece of Allah's creation.

The cow's milk is not merely a source of sustenance; it is a treasure trove of nutrients that fuel our bodies and minds. Rich in calcium, protein, vitamin D, and other essential vitamins and minerals, it plays a vital role in building strong bones, maintaining healthy muscles, and supporting the body's overall well-being. Allah, in His infinite wisdom, has designed this seemingly simple liquid to be a complete and balanced nutritional powerhouse.

What about honey, the healing liquid?

The Humble Honeybee

Allah, the Great, guided the honeybee to build their nests high up in the branches of trees. What is the reason? It's not just a residence, it's a factory as well. And the production is the Liquid Gold, The Healing for the Humankind. Allah, the Exalted, has also guided the entire process, from the construction of the house to the location of the factory. Allah, the Exalted, provided guidance for every step in the creation of honey. Each honeybee in the factory is aware of the specific task assigned to them. Examining the life of a honeybee reveals that the creation of honey is truly a miraculous process. Picture the brain of these bees. Is it a dot? And the flawless functioning of this minuscule brain. This knowledge, coordination, and creative home design are all guided by divine instructions. Scientists claim that bees are inherently programmed for their roles. By whom was this genetic predisposition designed? Is it just a coincidence? Isn't that so? The Quran, 1400 years ago, refers to bees using feminine pronouns. What is the reason? It is the female bees who perform all of these tasks. Scientists have confirmed that female bees are responsible for completing all tasks in the factory. By examining the verses thoroughly, you will see that all the guidance in the work has been directly specified by our Creator, Allah, the Exalted. Allah (ﷻ) has commanded the bees to obey the directions and labour quietly. Does the honeybee anticipate recognition from us humans since all of her tireless work is done for our well-being and healing? Her sole action is "we acknowledge our Lord, we do not seek recognition, we are committed to obeying His commands and fulfilling our roles diligently".

وَأَوْحَىٰ رَبُّكَ إِلَى ٱلنَّحْلِ أَنِ ٱتَّخِذِى مِنَ ٱلْجِبَالِ بُيُوتًا وَمِنَ ٱلشَّجَرِ وَمِمَّا
يَعْرِشُونَ ﴿٦٨﴾

ثُمَّ كُلِى مِن كُلِّ ٱلثَّمَرَٰتِ فَٱسْلُكِى سُبُلَ رَبِّكِ ذُلُلًا ۚ يَخْرُجُ مِنۢ بُطُونِهَا
شَرَابٌ مُّخْتَلِفٌ أَلْوَٰنُهُۥ فِيهِ شِفَآءٌ لِّلنَّاسِ ۗ إِنَّ فِى ذَٰلِكَ لَءَايَةً لِّقَوْمٍ
يَتَفَكَّرُونَ ﴿٦٩﴾

ثُمَّ كُلِى مِن كُلِّ ٱلثَّمَرَٰتِ فَٱسْلُكِى سُبُلَ رَبِّكِ ذُلُلًا ۚ يَخْرُجُ مِنۢ بُطُونِهَا
شَرَابٌ مُّخْتَلِفٌ أَلْوَٰنُهُۥ فِيهِ شِفَآءٌ لِّلنَّاسِ ۗ إِنَّ فِى ذَٰلِكَ لَءَايَةً لِّقَوْمٍ
يَتَفَكَّرُونَ ﴿٦٩﴾

Sahih International
And your Lord inspired to the bee, "Take for yourself among the mountains, houses, and among the trees and [in] that which they construct."

Sahih International
Then eat from all the fruits and follow the ways of your Lord laid down [for you]." There emerges from their bellies a drink, varying in colours, in which there is healing for people. Indeed, in that is a sign for a people who give thought.

Sahih International
And Allah (ﷻ), The Exalted created you; then He will take you in death. And among you is he who is reversed to the most decrepit [old] age so that he will not know, after [having had] knowledge, a thing. Indeed, Allah (ﷻ), The Exalted is Knowing and Competent.

Quran 16:68-70

Observe the verses where Allah (ﷻ) says "Your Lord"; do you not perceive the affection?

Continuing to contemplate each of Allah's (ﷻ) creations will help us understand the perfection of His creation. Subhan Allah (ﷻ). He simply didn't create us and expect us to worship Him in this world. He made us and made the Best for Us. He provided us with guidance. His infinite Mercy allows Him to always forgive us, no matter how great our sins are. Never underestimate the vastness of Allah's Forgiveness.

Jabir Ibn Abdullah reported: A man came to the Prophet, peace and blessings be upon him, and he said, "O my sins! O my sins!" The Prophet said to him, "Say: O Allah, your forgiveness is vaster than my sins, and your mercy is more hopeful to me than my deeds." The man said it, then the Prophet said, "Repeat it." The man repeated it, then the Prophet said, "Repeat it again." The man repeated it, then the Prophet said, "Stand up, for Allah (ﷻ), The Exalted has forgiven you."

Source: Shu'ab al-Imān 6622

Grade: Sahih (authentic) according to Al-Suyuti.

Chapter 8

Mission Bigger Than Me

* * *

When you want something, all the universe conspires in helping you to achieve it.

– Paulo Coelho

The mission is bigger than me. This was a common phrase used by my teacher when teaching us the Quran. Many times, I would wonder how my teacher knew what was happening in my home, as she would explain the verses in a way that connected to our lives.

There was wisdom in her words, and I slowly realised that these were the things that Allah (ﷻ), The Exalted wanted me to hear and learn. Subhan Allah. Many times, these words shook me because they were true. We often focus on things that occupy our valuable thoughts.

Iblis was a Jinn who worshipped Allah (ﷻ), The Exalted SWT and reached high ranks due to his intense worship. When Allah (ﷻ), The Exalted decided to create humans as successors and he was informing the Angels, Iblis was present with the Angels, which clearly shows he was honoured. However, he was eventually cursed. Why? Because for him it was **"Me bigger than the mission"**. His downfall was his focus on himself, thinking "me, me, me." He questioned why he should bow to Adam (May peace be upon Him), created from clay, while he was created from fire. His self-centredness led to his downfall, and he was cast out from the mercy of Allah (ﷻ) as he was not in a state of seeking forgiveness from our merciful Lord who can forgive any tyrant.

Gratitude is the opposite of egocentricity and self-centredness.

Looking back at the story of Iblis and Adam (May peace be upon Him), we see how easily one can get trapped in the idea of **"Me bigger than the Mission."** Without gratitude, we can easily fall into the snare of the ego and forget our purpose.

Gratitude is a quality that is highly encouraged in Islam. The Quran mentions the word "Shukr" (gratitude) around 70 times, indicating its importance. Gratitude is not just about saying **"Alhamdulillah"** when good things happen, but it is a state of being that should permeate our entire existence. As described in the Sufi tradition, gratitude encompasses both an internal disposition of the heart and an external expression in one's actions. (Khalil, 2016)

What is the mission? It is about spreading goodness, peace, and worshipping your Lord without comparing Him to any of His creations. The mission is not limited to being a scholar or a teacher who educates children on the Quran or a speaker who delivers grand speeches. While these roles are important, the mission is to live every aspect of our life in a state of gratitude and servitude to our Creator (Khalil, 2016).

As the Quran states, "And if you should count the favours of Allah, you could not enumerate them. Indeed, mankind is [generally] most unjust and ungrateful." [16:18]

The mission also encompasses simple acts like smiling at your loved ones, speaking kindly, and helping the needy with kind words. It involves cooking healthy meals for your family, maintaining a clean home, instilling values in your children, and caring for your parents as a duty prescribed by Allah.

The mission includes controlling your anger, practicing patience during tough times, and making efforts to overcome negative thoughts that may lead you astray. It is about understanding that every action, no matter how small, can be a part of fulfilling your purpose and pleasing your Lord. Instead of questioning why you have to do certain tasks or feeling unappreciated by others, shift your perspective to see these actions as a way to serve a higher purpose and seek the pleasure of Allah (ﷻ).

I could discuss this topic at length, but I'll move on to the next instead.

How the ME overcomes its mission.
What is the reason for me to cook all the time?
What is the reason for me to consistently clean?
Why do I need to be the one to always initiate contact with my family if they never reach out?
What is the reason my partner doesn't value me?
What is the reason for my children not loving me? I am not respected by them.
Why isn't my boss recognising the effort I put in?
Why am I the one facing this situation, why is it always me experiencing this?
Is it possible to connect this to the ideas of Iblis?

In some way, correct? Yes, this is how he will gradually retrieve you from your task. If we can control and change our thoughts here, we can overpower him, how?

By choosing positive thoughts and focusing on the greater mission, you can combat stress and negativity. Remember, the power lies in your ability to choose one thought over another. Embrace the idea that your everyday actions, no matter how mundane they may seem, are contributing to a larger mission that transcends your individual desires and concerns. Stay committed to doing your best in all aspects of your life, knowing that you are fulfilling a greater purpose and seeking the pleasure of your Creator.

Maintaining a grateful heart and focusing on the mission will protect you from the traps of ego and selfishness.

By cultivating an attitude of gratitude, you can overcome the **"me-centred"** mindset that leads to discontentment and resentment.

As long as we are alive, we have a purpose in this world. It is important to **Recognise, Reflect, and Renew.**.

As a student of Quran Tafseer, most of our homework was to reflect on the Ayah of the Qur'an. How these verses are connected to our life, what are the lessons we need to study and implement. When we are talking about mission, it's very important to go through the lessons of the prophets whose path we have to follow.

وَلَقَدۡ بَعَثۡنَا فِي كُلِّ أُمَّةٖ رَّسُولًا أَنِ ٱعۡبُدُواْ ٱللَّهَ وَٱجۡتَنِبُواْ
ٱلطَّٰغُوتَۖ فَمِنۡهُم مَّنۡ هَدَى ٱللَّهُ وَمِنۡهُم مَّنۡ حَقَّتۡ عَلَيۡهِ
ٱلضَّلَٰلَةُۚ فَسِيرُواْ فِي ٱلۡأَرۡضِ فَٱنظُرُواْ كَيۡفَ كَانَ عَٰقِبَةُ
ٱلۡمُكَذِّبِينَ ٣٦

Sahih International
And We certainly sent into every nation a messenger, [saying], "Worship Allah (ﷻ), The Exalted and avoid Taghut." And among them were those whom Allah (ﷻ), The Exalted guided, and among them were those upon whom error was [deservedly] decreed. So proceed through the earth and observe how the end of the deniers was.

Quran 16:36

Remember Ibrahim (May peace be upon him), known as the Friend of Allah (ﷻ), a small young boy who was thrown into the fire by his own father and his own community. What emotional pain and humiliation he must have endured! As per Ibn Kathir (RA) in his book The Prophets, when they started to tie him with chains, he remembered Allah (ﷻ) by uttering the words: "La ilaha illa anta, Subhanaka Rabbil-'Alameen, lakal Hamd walakal Mulk, la shareeka lak." "There is no deity but You, You are glorified, O' Lord of the worlds. To You belongs all praise and dominion. You have no partner." When Ibrahim (AS) was tied with chains, placed on the catapult and thrown into the fire, he said: "HasbunAllah wa nay'mal wakeel. HasbunAllah, wa nay'mal wakeel. Allah is Sufficient for us, how good a Protector He is."

Ibn 'Asakir reported in his history book that Abu Ya'la narrated from Abu Hurayrah that the Prophet (may peace be upon Him) said, "When Ibraheem was thrown into the fire, he said, 'O Allah, You are One in the sky and I am one on the earth, and I worship you.' Some of the (pious) predecessors mentioned that when Ibraheem (AS) was in the air after being thrown, Angel Jibreel came to him and said, 'O Ibraheem, do you have any need?' He replied, 'From you? No.' Ibn 'Abbas and Sa'eed ibn Jubayr said that the angel of rain said, 'When will I be commanded so that I could send down rain?' However, Allah's order was quicker. The people wanted to prevail and be victorious, but they were humiliated instead. Similarly, they wanted to overpower him, but they were overpowered. Allah (ﷻ) said, 'Then they looked for a way to plan against him, so We made them losers.' And in another verse, the word used is (Qur'an 21:70). So they gained nothing but loss and humiliation in this world. And as for the Hereafter, their fire will not be cool or safe on them. Similarly, they will not be greeted and spoken to with a soft speech. Rather, it will be, as Allah (ﷻ) said, 'Evil indeed is that dwelling place and as an abode.' (Qur'an 25:66)

When Ibraheem (as) shunned his people and migrated for Allah's sake, without a child and with his wife who was barren, and along with them his nephew Loot (AS) ibn Haran ibn Azar, Allah (ﷻ) granted him later on pious children and made in his progeny Prophethood and the Book. Every Prophet who was sent after him was from his progeny. Similarly, every book that was revealed after him was revealed to one of his progenies. All this was an honour and favour from Allah (ﷻ) to Ibraheem for having left his country, family, and close relatives, and having migrated to a land wherein he could worship his Lord (swt) and wherein he could invite people to the worship of Allah (ﷻ) alone.

Did his test stop there? No, he then had to go through many tests harder than this. But at any point was he drowned by the thought of me, my pain, my heart, my child, my wife, my family, my father? Absolutely a big no.

Mission was **From Allah (ﷻ) for Allah (ﷻ) and To Allah (ﷻ)**, Rest all was for the sake of Allah (ﷻ).

Prophet Lut (May peace be upon him) was the nephew of Ibrahim (May peace be upon him). When I hear many people complaining about their children, spouse, or family members, the name of Prophet Lut (AS) often comes to mind. Lut (AS), upon the instruction of Ibrahim (AS), went to Sodom, the main city in that region. The inhabitants of Sodom were extremely evil, immoral, and insolent. They openly engaged in shameful acts instead of forbidding evil. Prophet Lut (AS) invited them to the path of righteousness and obedience to Allah, the

Exalted, but they rejected the call and persisted in their transgressions, disbelief, and rebelliousness. As a result, Allah (ﷻ) destroyed them with a punishment so severe that it had not been seen before, making them an example of what can happen to a people who persist in disobedience and disbelief. Anyone who came after them was meant to learn from their fate, and Allah (ﷻ) mentioned their story in clear terms in various places.

Now, even though Lut (AS) was a prophet, his wife did not believe in him, and she was also punished along with the others. Similarly, Prophet Nuh's son did not believe in him, causing him great pain. We can relate to this, as we often focus on our children and expect only good from them. Sisters and brothers, this is the case of a prophet, one who received direct revelations from the Creator of the Heavens and the Earth, Allah (ﷻ). It is not a joke that his own son did not believe. We should not assume that the parenting of a prophet was not perfect or that they did not take care of their children. They are prophets, chosen by Allah (ﷻ).

I have heard mothers blaming themselves, thinking there is fault in my upbringing. If you have played your role to the best of your ability, pleasing Allah, the Exalted, then you have passed the right message to your children. And if they turn away, remember the story of Prophet Nuh (AS). We are here with a clear mission, so let us focus on that rather than dwelling on worldly concerns.

Prophet Musa (Alayhi Salaam) (May peace be upon him), Ya Rabb, I am truly intrigued by the special love Allah (ﷻ) had for this prominent prophet, that He spoke to him directly. The Quran mentions Moses more than any other prophet, with his name appearing 136 times, and his life being recounted in greater detail than that of any other.

Whenever I read the verses where Allah (ﷻ) asks, "And has there come to you the story of Moses?", I feel a sense of a parent tenderly addressing their beloved child. As a mother, we are filled with pride when speaking of our children. However, I cannot compare the love of a parent for a child to Allah's (ﷻ) boundless love.

Umar ibn al-Khattab reported: Some prisoners of war were brought to the Prophet, peace and blessings be upon him, and a nursing woman was among them. Whenever she found a child among the prisoners, she would take it to her chest and nurse it. The Prophet said to us, "Do you think this woman would throw her child into the fire?" We said, "No, not if she was able to stop it." The Prophet said, "Allah (ﷻ), The Exalted is more merciful to His servants than this mother is to her child."

Source: Sahih al-Bukhari 5999, Sahih Al-Muslim 2754

Musa (Alahi salaam) (AS) when Allah (ﷻ) the exalted asked him to go to Pharaoh with a bigger mission, that Pharaoh who was a tyrant at the peak of his cruelty, the newborn babies were slaughtered.

Allah (ﷻ) the Almighty revealed: These are Verses of the manifest Book (that make clear truth from falsehood, good from evil, etc.). We recite to you some of the news of Moses and Pharaoh in truth, for a people who believe (those who believe in this Qur'an, and in the Oneness of Allah). Verily, Pharaoh exalted himself in the land and made its people sects, weakening (oppressing) a group (i.e. children of Israel) among them, killing their sons, and letting their females live. Verily, he was of the Mufsideen (i.e., those who commit great sins and crimes, oppressors, tyrants, etc.).

And with a mission ahead.

"Go, both of you, to Pharaoh, verily, he has transgressed (all bounds in disbelief and disobedience and behaved arrogantly and as a tyrant). And speak to him mildly, perhaps he may accept admonition or fear Allah."

We have a lesson in these verses. See how Allah (ﷻ) says to speak to a tyrant mildly. What about us? Even to our near ones, how do we speak?

They said, "Our Lord! Verily! We fear lest he should hasten to punish us or lest he should transgress (all bounds against us)."

He Allah (ﷻ) said, "Fear not, Verily! I am with you both, Hearing and Seeing. So go you both to him, and say: 'Verily, we are Messengers of your Lord, so let the children of Israel go with us, and torment them not; indeed, we have come with a sign from your Lord! And peace will be upon him who follows the guidance! Truly, it has been revealed to us that the torment will be for him who denies, believes not in the Oneness of Allah (ﷻ) and in His Messengers, etc., and turns away' (from the truth and obedience of Allah)." Surah 20:25-48

Musa (Alahi salaam) and his brother Harun went to Pharaoh despite their fear. Yet, Musa (Alahi salaam) did not stop his mission. You all know the story of Musa (Alahi salaam), who was raised in Pharaoh's palace. Did he have doubts, thinking, "Oh, how will I call him to the right path? I have to be grateful to them. I can't take this further. What will they think of me? How can I be ungrateful? Isn't it bad? What if he kills me?" Many of us can relate to such thoughts. But Musa (Alahi salaam) focused on his mission - the greater calling to guide people to the right path, the path of Allah(ﷻ). People may call you a stranger, mock your way of talking, dressing, or living, but put your complete trust in Allah(ﷻ).

When Pharaoh's oppression intensified, the divine command came for Musa (Alahi salaam) to leave Egypt with the Children of Israel, in secret. When Pharaoh found out, he gathered a great army to catch up with Musa (Alahi salaam) and his people before they reached Palestine. Pharaoh and his troops set out, leaving behind their gardens and wealth. They caught up with Musa (Alahi salaam) and his people at sunrise, on the shores of the Red Sea.

Imagine being in Musa (Alahi salaam)'s place, leading a group of people with a powerful enemy behind you. You are facing a sea that is 2,250 km long and 355 km wide. The people who have left all their belongings behind, trusting you, are now screaming, "What now? We are caught, the enemy is going to kill us!" We often panic in such situations, even over a simple phone call at an odd time. He never knew the 2250 km long sea is going to split open for him. But he knew that his Lord, Allah, the Exalted, was enough for him. That is the point where we need to be, and that is the point where miracles happen. And so it happened, marked into history for generations to witness, the moment Musa (Alahi salaam) said.

> ***When the two groups came face to face, the companions of Moses cried out, "We are overtaken for sure." (61) Moses reassured them, "Absolutely not! My Lord is certainly with me—He will guide me." (62)***

This moment turned out to be a time of miracle. Allah (ﷻ), The Exalted could have split the river and prepared it before Musa (Alahi salaam) and the people arrived, but why did He wait for Musa (Alahi salaam) to express his faith? Indeed, that was a testing moment to know the pure love of His slave towards Him. And here we are discussing it, having a clear lesson. What happens to us most of the time is that when we reach such moments, we panic and fail. Then, what miracles do we expect? Instead, place complete trust in your Lord, and you will witness miracles in your life.

> *Then We inspired to Moses, "Strike with your staff the sea," and it parted, and each portion was like a great towering mountain.*
> *And We advanced thereto the pursuers.*
> *And We saved Moses and those with him, all together.*

Then We drowned the others.
Indeed, in that is a sign, but most of them were not to be believers.

This is the crucial moment, my readers. This is the time when you are on a mission, when each of your actions is intended to be part of spreading goodness and forbidding evil - the basic concept of Islam. Have complete trust in Allah (ﷻ) and then you will have no fear, no regrets, and no pains.

Chapter 20: Taa-Haa, Verse 46
Allah (ﷻ), The Exalted reassured them, "Have no fear! I am with you, hearing and seeing." (46)

When we examine the stories of other prophets, we realise there were moments in their lives where Allah (ﷻ) tested them, and they succeeded. They never complained to Allah (ﷻ); instead, they made du'a (supplications) to seek the strength and guidance to face those challenges.

Our beloved Prophet had to endure numerous hardships. While still in his mother's womb, he lost his father at just six months. When he was six years old, he lost his mother, and at the age of eight, he lost his grandfather, who had been caring for him. Even when he was chosen as the Prophet of Allah (ﷻ) and faced a daunting mission ahead, his own people turned against him. They started hurting him, his family, and his companions. They mocked him, laughed at him, and even went so far as to try to kill him and his companions. Yet, all these hardships were endured for the sake of Islam. If we reflect on the life of our Beloved Prophet, we will understand that it was too much for an ordinary person to handle, but he never uttered a word that displeased Allah (ﷻ).

Difficult times are part of Allah's laws in this universe; they are tests that people must endure.

Do people think they will be left alone and they will not be tried?... (Al-`Ankbut 29:3)

Do you suppose that you will enter Paradise untouched by the suffering endured by the people who passed before you?

They were afflicted by the misery and hardship, and they were so convulsed that the Messenger and the believers with him cried out, "When will Allah's help arrive?" (Al-Baqarah 2: 214)

When you claim to believe in Allah (ﷻ), stand for what is right, oppose what is wrong, support justice, or fight oppression, these commitments will all be tested. Allah (ﷻ) will discern who is truthful and who is lying.

This is the tradition of those on the straight path at all times. The Prophet and his companions were asked in the Qur'an a question that is also posed to all of us:

Our mission is greater than ourselves, sisters and brothers. Let us gain a clearer understanding of it.

> *Patience is not sitting and waiting; it is foreseeing. It is looking at the thorn and seeing the rose, looking at the night and seeing the day. Lovers are patient and know that the moon needs time to become full.*
>
> *–Rumi*

Chapter 9

The Hidden Treasure – Your Powerhouse

* * *

"The human heart has hidden treasures, in secret kept, in silence sealed."

- Charlotte Brontë.

Finally unearthing your Treasure. It's your Heart. Why Heart? Let's see,

Treasure - As per Wikipedia, is a concentration of wealth often originating from ancient history that is considered lost and/or forgotten until discovered.

We are here to unearth our treasure - our heart.

A 312-gram size which beats 60-80 per minute, about 40 million beats per year. In every beat, about one-quarter pound of blood enters the heart, and it pumps 2200 gallons of blood every day, about 56 million gallons during a lifetime. Do you give any maintenance for this machine of yours? Did you really know these numbers before? Do you have any discomfort because of this stupendous amount of work done every day? Do you feel it? Subhan Allah (ﷻ), The Exalted. All praise is due to Allah (ﷻ), The Exalted.

Whenever I ponder over these facts, the way how our organs function and it's very important to know it only if we will realise how specially we were created and nurtured. I feel I'm an ungrateful slave having these hidden blessings we always used to be ungrateful to our Lord who loves and cares for us most.

Most of my findings and studies are based on the great work of Scholar Imam Ibn Al Qayyim (May Allah's Mercy be upon him), The book which is translated into English by Capt. Anas Abdul-Hameed Al Qoz, "Men and the Universe." It's very important as a believer to go through this book once so that you can realise the wonderful human design.

Below are some facts mentioned by the great Imam:

If the heart were employed as a lifting machine, it would lift a weight of two pounds two feet high with the same effort that it uses to pulsate once.

The heart pumps 8000 litres of blood every day in the whole blood circulation, which extends to about 150 km throughout the tissues of the body, transferring blood loaded with nutrients and oxygen. To appreciate the vitality of the blood supply, it is enough to note that the brain will be irreversibly affected by a halt of oxygen supply for only five minutes.

Some of them deny and hold that the intellectual functions are in the head. The truth, however, seems to be that it starts from the heart, then finds its elaboration and fruition in the head. One may refer to the Quran to support this:

قُلْ مَن كَانَ عَدُوًّا لِّجِبْرِيلَ فَإِنَّهُۥ نَزَّلَهُۥ عَلَىٰ قَلْبِكَ بِإِذْنِ ٱللَّهِ
مُصَدِّقًا لِّمَا بَيْنَ يَدَيْهِ وَهُدًى وَبُشْرَىٰ لِلْمُؤْمِنِينَ ﴿٩٧﴾

Sahih International
Say, "Whoever is an enemy to Gabriel - it is [none but] he who has brought the Qur'an down ***upon your heart****, [O Muhammad], by permission of Allah (ﷻ), The Exalted, confirming that which was before it and as guidance and good tidings for the believers."*
Quran 2:97

From this verse, it's clear the storage of knowledge is in the HEART,

إِذْ هَمَّت طَّآئِفَتَانِ مِنكُمْ أَن تَفْشَلَا وَٱللَّهُ وَلِيُّهُمَا ۗ وَعَلَى ٱللَّهِ
فَلْيَتَوَكَّلِ ٱلْمُؤْمِنُونَ ﴿١٢٢﴾

Muhsin Khan
When two parties from among you were about to lose heart, but Allah (ﷻ), The Exalted was their Wali (Supporter and Protector). And in Allah (ﷻ), The Exalted should the believers put their trust.
Quran 3:122

فَلَوْلَآ إِذْ جَآءَهُم بَأْسُنَا تَضَرَّعُوا۟ وَلَٰكِن قَسَتْ قُلُوبُهُمْ وَزَيَّنَ لَهُمُ
ٱلشَّيْطَٰنُ مَا كَانُوا۟ يَعْمَلُونَ ﴿٤٣﴾

Sahih International
Then why, when Our punishment came to them, did they not humble themselves? But their hearts became hardened, and Satan made attractive to them that which they were doing.
Quran 6:43

From this verse we understand how important is to keep our heart in safe locker. We will come to this point later deeply.

وَأَمَّا ٱلَّذِينَ فِى قُلُوبِهِم مَّرَضٌ فَزَادَتْهُمْ رِجْسًا إِلَىٰ رِجْسِهِمْ
وَمَاتُوا۟ وَهُمْ كَـٰفِرُونَ ﴿١٢٥﴾

Sahih International
But as for those in whose hearts is disease, it has [only] increased them in evil [in addition] to their evil. And they will have died while they are disbelievers..

Quran 9:125

يَـٰٓأَيُّهَا ٱلنَّاسُ قَدْ جَآءَتْكُم مَّوْعِظَةٌ مِّن رَّبِّكُمْ وَشِفَآءٌ لِّمَا فِى
ٱلصُّدُورِ وَهُدًى وَرَحْمَةٌ لِّلْمُؤْمِنِينَ ﴿٥٧﴾

Yusuf Ali
O mankind! there hath come to you a direction from your Lord and a healing for the (diseases) in your hearts,- and for those who believe, a guidance and a Mercy.

Quran 10:57

ثُمَّ بَعَثْنَا مِنۢ بَعْدِهِۦ رُسُلًا إِلَىٰ قَوْمِهِمْ فَجَآءُوهُم بِٱلْبَيِّنَـٰتِ فَمَا كَانُوا۟
لِيُؤْمِنُوا۟ بِمَا كَذَّبُوا۟ بِهِۦ مِن قَبْلُ ۚ كَذَٰلِكَ نَطْبَعُ عَلَىٰ قُلُوبِ ٱلْمُعْتَدِينَ ﴿٧٤﴾

Sahih International
Then We sent after him messengers to their peoples, and they came to them with clear proofs. But they were not to believe in that which they had denied before. Thus We seal over the hearts of the transgressors.

Quran 10:74

ٱلَّذِينَ ءَامَنُوا۟ وَتَطْمَئِنُّ قُلُوبُهُم بِذِكْرِ ٱللَّهِ ۗ أَلَا بِذِكْرِ ٱللَّهِ تَطْمَئِنُّ ٱلْقُلُوبُ ﴿٢٨﴾

Sahih International
Those who have believed and whose hearts are assured by the remembrance of Allah (ﷻ), The Exalted. Unquestionably, by the remembrance of Allah hearts are assured."

Quran 13:28

The Quran frequently uses the term "Qalb" (Heart), which appears 132 times, and at times substitutes it with similar terms.

Why the heart and not any other organ in our body? Why 132 times? If your creator has to mention it, then there are deep reasons behind it. This led me to research on the importance of our little organ and its role in our life, and I found that it was my treasure. Now, what about yours? Think, ponder, and renew.

As per Gregg Braden, the author, scientist, on his

Every human heart has 40,000 specialised cells which create a neural network in the heart, brain-like cells but they are not in the brain, they are in the heart so-called "little brain in the heart." These 40,000 specialised cells are called sensory neurons. What scientists discovered is that these cells think independently of the cranial brain. They feel and remember independently of the cranial brain. When I am experiencing a good moment, seeing something, hearing something, I am registering it in two places: in my mind, in my cranial mind, and as well as in my heart. Similarly, if we experience trauma, it gets registered in two places as well. What's heart intelligence? According to scientists, the neural network in the heart is linked to wisdom, to an intelligence that is right for us, so basically, it means your heart communicates with you what's right for you, mine for me, yours for you. So, as said, when you are in a situation, as a believer, I can say what's wrong and what's right? What my Lord loves, what He hates, ask your heart. Before you do anything, ask your heart, is it right, will Allah (ﷻ), The Exalted be pleased with me if I do this or will He get upset? I am sure you are going to get the answer.

I have been seeing Mr. Gregg Braden's presentations and going through the articles which are published on GAIA.com. It's not only about the mysteries of the heart; several topics on human design and how we function amazed me. The fact that The Quran, revealed 1400 years ago, has stated so clearly. Open your eyes, look into the world, gain knowledge, ponder over the signs because that's very important for you and me to be firm in our faith, to love our creator. When you love Him, obeying Him, worshipping Him becomes not a ritual but the precious moments of love, and you will yearn for it.

As per Gregg in his presentation of Brain and Heart Coherence, some major points are as follows. Every moment and every day, there is a conversation between the heart and the brain. Our heart is sending signals to the brain, and based on that, the brain releases the chemistry to the body. So if we get stressed, enraged, angry, fearful, hateful, or frustrated, the heart sends signals to the brain. These signals are irregular, which the brain sends the stress chemistry to the body. It's good for some way, some time, but not always. As per the HeartMath Institute in Northern California, they are conducting several research studies to learn about the heart apart from just being a blood-pumping machine in the body. When a human is indulging in gratitude, compassion, love, care, and appreciation, the signals that the heart sends to the brain are smooth, and the brain feels safe, so the brain doesn't need to release the stress chemistry. Thus, it releases anti-ageing hormones and a powerful immune response to our body. This is called heart-brain coherence. Coherence is a low-level frequency, a safe communication, similar to the way that whales communicate in the oceans. 0.10 hertz is the optimum low-frequency coherence. So if we can create the feelings in our heart, for example, a frequency of 0.10 hertz between our heart and the brain that begins releasing signals to our body, it has been documented to have several benefits. It reduces blood pressure, reduces the chances of stroke, and increases the immune system. When we are able to feel these feelings such as compassion, gratitude, appreciation, love, forgiveness, sustained for a long period of time, the immune system increases the DHEA level. It's a precaution to all hormones in the body. DHEA (Dehydroepiandrosterone) increases by 100 percent in 3 minutes by only feeling the feeling of compassion, appreciation, love, gratitude, and such, while the stress chemistry can reduce the DHEA level by 23 percent at the same time. So let's see the role of DHEA.

As per the various studies, a decrease in DHEA is seen for those categories.

The people with heart disease, metabolic syndrome, depression, osteoporosis, obesity, erectile dysfunction, ageing, HIV, menopause, inflammatory bowel disease, and much more.

So it's clear that these feelings are the qualities that the body needs to heal itself. The bodies are designed in a way to heal themselves, and our own science has now shown that every cell, every organ in our body has the ability to heal itself. Even the organs we have been told cannot heal, such as brain tissues, heart tissues, spinal cord tissues, pancreatic tissues, all heal under the right conditions and the right environment. Science couldn't understand these facts for some time, but now scientific research has validated that we may create within our own bodies the powerful emotions, the heart-based emotions that begin healing our body.

So by healing the anger, forgiving someone who did terrible things to you, leaving the grudges from your heart, filling your heart with peace, love, compassion, gratitude, trust in your Lord, you are creating a coherence between your heart and brain which is going to heal your body, keeping your body and soul fit, at peace. No tensions, no regrets, no complaints. Every moment, every day is the moment of gratitude. Hope you can connect to the point why.

Prophet Muhammad (ﷺ) said,
Beware! There is a piece of flesh in the body if it becomes good (reformed) the whole body becomes good but if it gets spoilt the whole body gets spoilt and that is the heart.

– Sahih al-Bukhari 52

Abu Sa'id reported: The Messenger of Allah, peace and blessings be upon him, said:

There are four kinds of hearts: a polished heart as shiny as a radiant lamp, a sealed heart with a knot tied around it, a heart that is turned upside down, and a heart that is wrapped. As for the polished heart, it is the heart of the believer and its lamp is the light of faith. The sealed heart is the heart of the unbeliever. The heart that is turned upside down is the heart of a pure hypocrite, for he had knowledge but he denied it. As for the heart that is wrapped, it is the heart that contains both faith and hypocrisy. The parable of faith in this heart is the parable of the herb that is sustained by pure water, and the parable of the hypocrisy in it is the parable of an ulcer that thrives upon pus and blood; whichever of the two is greater will dominate.

Source: Musnad Ahmad 11129, Grade: Sahih

Now speaking about the Heart and its mysteries, I hope to include it in my upcoming book, In shaa Allah. Concluding for now, I am sure we all have realised what's our treasure. Now, once we find our treasure, what are we supposed to do with it? Protect it, right? If we look into the world, how treasures like gold, diamonds are kept in safe lockers, dust-free, not accessible to everyone, right? Precious gems kept for display in museums are under bulletproof glass. Security guards are placed around the clock. What are you and I supposed to do with our treasure? Expose it to such conditions where it can collect dust? Allowing open access for anyone to enter and seize it? Place it in those situations, fill it with those factors that can deteriorate it? No, we are going to keep it in safe locks, protected away from dust and with limited access. Guard it with good thoughts, remembrance of your Lord, enrich it with The Quran, and you can always keep it under safe locks.

What happens when the burner is clogged? If the burner is not cleaned regularly, grease and other cooking residue can build up, clogging the burner and reducing the flow of gas.

Then many of you must be experienced with such a burner. If you keep your pots on it, they turn black. Why? When the fuel does not burn completely, a sooty flame appears, which makes the bottom of the utensil black. This happens because the air holes are getting blocked, and the fuel does not burn completely.

Now let's compare our heart to the burner. Think of the heart, which is clogged with doubts, negative thoughts, jealousy, hatred, desires, expectations from people, and much more. If our heart is clogged like a burner, what happens? If it becomes clogged with doubts, negative thoughts, jealousy, hatred, desires, and unrealistic expectations, the consequences can be just as detrimental. Just as a clogged burner can blacken a beautiful pot with its fumes, a heart burdened by such internal blockages can inadvertently hurt those around us and spread negativity. Just as it is essential to regularly clean our burners, it is crucial that we remove these clogs from our hearts. Only then can what we say and do truly reflect the purity and goodness within us.

As we regularly make sure we clean the stove, we have to make sure to have regular self-check on our heart.

Abdullah ibn Mas'ud reported: The Messenger of Allah, peace and blessings be upon him, said:

> *O Allah, bring our hearts together, reconcile between us, guide us to ways of peace, and deliver us from darkness into light. Keep us away from immorality, outwardly and inwardly, and bless us in our hearing, our seeing, our hearts, our spouses, and our children. Accept our repentance, for You alone are the Relenting, the Merciful. Make us grateful for Your blessings, praising and accepting them, and give them to us in full.*
>
> *Source: Sunan Abī Dāwūd 968, Grade: Sahih*

Chapter 10

The Everest Goal: Conquering Your Everest

* * *

Don't waste time collecting other people's autographs; rather devote it to making your own autograph worth collecting.

George Bernard Shaw

What about climbing up the tallest mountain on the planet? Yes, Mount Everest. Have any of you, including me, thought of attempting it? I haven't yet. Even just to the 14th floor of my office building, I can sometimes feel the effects of the change in altitude, as my ears will occasionally become blocked during the short elevator ride that takes less than 3 minutes. I can only imagine the profound physical and mental strain that would come with attempting to scale the mighty Everest.

Now what about climbing a mountain of 8849 metres (29,032 feet). It's not a piece of cake… Imagine standing at the foot of Mount Everest, its snow-capped peak piercing the sky, a symbol of immense challenge and unimaginable beauty. That, my friends, is the Everest Goal - the ultimate aspiration that calls to your very soul. It's not just about reaching the summit, it's about the journey, the growth, the resilience you cultivate along the way.

Everest climbers have to go through months of preparation physically and mentally. When it comes to terms of risks, as we know, not every climber comes back from the expedition. That's the path they need to choose, which is filled with life or death. Reaching the summit is not predictable due to the high risks involved. At 29,032 feet above sea level, the air is 33% less dense, which means it takes three breaths to receive the same volume of oxygen that you take in one breath at your home. Sounds easy? No, right?

Surviving at high altitudes is no easy feat for humans. Yet, what compels them to choose the less travelled path? The path fraught with challenges, the path between life and death, the path of nature's unexpected surprises. Despite the harshness of the environment, those with unwavering determination and resilience make the difficult choice to pursue their goal.

Everest, with its treacherous slopes, unpredictable weather, and unforgiving terrain, represents the myriad challenges we face in life. It's the embodiment of adversity, the ultimate test of endurance, a journey where every step demands unwavering determination and a deep understanding of our own limits.

When I went through the book "Into Thin Air" by Jon Krakauer, one of the survivors of the 1996 Mount Everest disaster, I was shocked with fear at some moments. I felt like I was somewhere on Everest.

Many of you must have read it. If not, I suggest you please read this book which will give you a clear picture of how hard it is to reach the summit. The disaster that took eight climbers' lives. When Mr. Jon in his books explains the struggles and risks that they take to achieve their goal, I was moved by the fact of how far humans can reach for their goal.

One of them in the team along with Jon was Mr. Beck Weathers, one of the American pathologists who survived the 1996 disaster but was left with great health challenges. His right arm was amputated halfway between the elbow and wrist. All four fingers and his thumb on his left hand were also amputated, as well as parts of both feet. His nose was amputated and reconstructed with tissue from his ear and forehead.

The autobiography book of Mr. Beck Weathers, "Left for Dead," delivers several important messages, primarily about survival, resilience, and personal transformation. His story is a powerful testament to the strength of the human spirit. His miraculous survival despite extreme cold and injuries underscores the extraordinary willpower and endurance of the human body and mind.

The book highlights how close encounters with death can spark profound self-reflection and personal change. Weathers uses his Everest experience as a catalyst to reassess his life, values, and priorities. It shows that facing mortality can lead to transformation and a renewed sense of purpose.

> *"Your body doesn't carry you up there. Your mind does. Your body is exhausted hours before you reach the top; it is only through will and focus and drive that you continue to move. If you lose that focus, your body is a dead, worthless thing beneath you."*
>
> *- Beck Weathers,*
> *Left for Dead: My Journey Home from Everest.*

After going through all these testimonies, I was interested in learning the duration for which one can stay at the summit to enjoy the amazing view.

Climbers typically stay at Mount Everest's summit point for 15 to 30 minutes, dealing with several critical factors. If they insist on staying beyond this period, there is a high chance of them developing high altitude sickness, losing their energy levels drastically, and being unable to descend. Additionally, the weather at the summit can change rapidly at any unexpected moment.

So that's it? An expedition that took almost 6 weeks from the base camp to the Everest summit and you are supposed to have moments of joy for 15-30 minutes. It's not just about reaching the peak, it's also about the knowledge you bring back from the journey.

Our own lives are similar journeys. We each have a personal Everest, a goal that demands our unwavering commitment, our resilience, and our ability to push past perceived limitations. This Everest might be the pursuit of a dream career, the healing of a broken heart, the overcoming of a deeply rooted fear, or even the journey toward spiritual enlightenment.

The climbers who scale Everest are not merely adventurers; they are individuals like you and me who have tapped into an extraordinary strength within themselves, ready to go for that extra mile, a source of resilience that empowers them to conquer their fears and achieve the seemingly impossible.

That "Extra mile" matters a lot.

But there are men for whom the unattainable has a special attraction. Usually, they are not experts; their ambitions and fantasies are strong enough to brush aside the doubts which more cautious men might have. Determination and faith are their strongest weapons. At best, such men are regarded as eccentric; at worst, mad...
Everest has attracted its share of men like these. Their mountaineering experience varied from none at all to very slight; certainly, none of them had the kind of experience that would make an ascent of Everest a reasonable goal. Three things they all had in common: faith in themselves, great determination, and endurance.

Walt Unsworth
Everest

I grew up with an ambition and determination without which I would have been a good deal happier. I thought a lot and developed the far away look of a dreamer, for it was always the distant heights which fascinated me and drew me to them in spirit. I was not sure what would be accomplished by means of tenacity and little else, but the target was set high and each rebuff only saw me more determined to see at least one major dream through its fulfillment.

Earl Denman
Alone to Everest

This Everest Goal, however, is not confined to physical mountains. It represents the grandest ambitions of your heart, the dreams that hold the power to ignite your spirit. It encompasses both the tangible and the intangible, the material and the spiritual, the aspirations you strive for in this world and the ultimate destination that lies beyond.

Defining your Everest Goal is a deeply personal. It requires a deep understanding of your values, your passions, and the purpose that truly resonates within you. Ask yourself: What truly matters to you? What legacy do you wish to leave behind? What dreams keep you awake at night, whispering promises of fulfillment?

This is where the concept of "Akhirah," the afterlife in Islamic belief, adds another layer of depth to this journey. The Akhirah, a realm of ultimate accountability and reward, serves as a powerful reminder of the bigger picture. It inspires us to align our actions and aspirations with a higher purpose, to seek fulfilment beyond fleeting pleasures and worldly achievements.

Remember, your Everest Goal is not static. It's a compass, guiding you through life's ever-changing terrain. It evolves with you, adapting to your experiences and your expanding understanding of yourself and the world.

When we are at the end of this journey, it's very important to have a clear goal and to prepare for it. For that, the path you choose must not be easy, yet we need to prepare for it,

As famous poet Robert Frost says in his masterpiece "The Road Not Taken,"

Two roads diverged in a wood, and I—

I took the one less traveled by,

And that has made all the difference.

Yes, that makes all the difference. You, too, have the capacity to conquer your own personal Everest. This journey, however, begins with a deep understanding of yourself. It requires you to look inward, to understand your motivations, your weaknesses, and your strengths. It's about identifying the unique talents and gifts that lie within you and utilising them to create a life of purpose and fulfilment.

As we try exploring the concept of "Mission Bigger Than Me," we are moving towards it. Think of your Everest Goal as a beacon, shining a light on the path ahead. As you set your sights on this grand aspiration, remember that the true reward lies in the journey itself. Embrace the challenges, learn from your mistakes, celebrate your victories, and never stop striving for growth.

The path to your Everest Goal may be arduous, filled with twists and turns, but the view from the summit, my friends, is worth every ounce of effort. The journey is not about reaching the top; it's about becoming the best version of yourself along the way. And that, my friends, is a victory worth celebrating. We may not have anyone to support; there will be people to discourage you, pull you down. But think about the view from the summit point.

As believers, we have to make wise choices. We have clear proofs, and we, as believers, know what our ultimate destination, "Akhirah," is. Prepare for it. We know the rewards, yet we don't want to pursue it?

مَّثَلُ ٱلْجَنَّةِ ٱلَّتِى وُعِدَ ٱلْمُتَّقُونَ ۖ فِيهَآ أَنْهَٰرٌ مِّن مَّآءٍ غَيْرِ ءَاسِنٍ وَأَنْهَٰرٌ مِّن لَّبَنٍ
لَّمْ يَتَغَيَّرْ طَعْمُهُۥ وَأَنْهَٰرٌ مِّنْ خَمْرٍ لَّذَّةٍ لِّلشَّٰرِبِينَ وَأَنْهَٰرٌ مِّنْ عَسَلٍ مُّصَفًّى ۖ
وَلَهُمْ فِيهَا مِن كُلِّ ٱلثَّمَرَٰتِ وَمَغْفِرَةٌ مِّن رَّبِّهِمْ ۖ كَمَنْ هُوَ خَٰلِدٌ فِى ٱلنَّارِ وَسُقُوا۟
مَآءً حَمِيمًا فَقَطَّعَ أَمْعَآءَهُمْ ﴿١٥﴾

Sahih International
Is the description of Paradise, which the righteous are promised, wherein are rivers of water unaltered, rivers of milk the taste of which never changes, rivers of wine delicious to those who drink, and rivers of purified honey, in which they will have from all kinds of fruits and forgiveness from their Lord, like those who abide eternally in the Fire and are given to drink scalding water that will sever their intestines?

Quran 47:15

Sahih International
So he will be in a pleasant life-
In an elevated garden,
It's [fruit] to be picked hanging near.
They will be told, "Eat and drink in satisfaction for what you put forth in the days past." Quran 69:21-24

"But those who believe and do deeds of righteousness, we shall soon admit them to gardens, with rivers flowing beneath, to dwell therein forever. Allah's promise is the truth, and whose word can be truer than Allah's?" (4:122)

The Holy Quran describes Jannah as "Gardens of Pleasure" prepared for the righteous believers to dwell in for eternity. It contains "all that the souls could desire, all that the eyes could delight in..." (43:71). Whoever attains Jannah has attained the "Supreme Success" (9:89).

This is not the words of the world, my dear sisters and brothers, but the words of Allah, the Exalted. These are the words Revealed from Heaven to the heart of the best man to ever walk the earth, Our beloved prophet Muhammad (May peace be upon him). This is no mere promise. For example, if you have an offer from your company to work on a very difficult project, you may need to sacrifice your sleep, your food, and your family life for a certain period of time. Yet, you will have a chance to settle in your dream country. What do you think? Definitely, many of us would work for it. However, this promise can be changed, as it is made by humans. If there are any unexpected challenges in between, you may finish the project but not end up getting the reward you expected. This is because it is the worldly life and worldly promises yet we are ready to work for it. The promise from Allah (ﷻ), The Exalted is "Haqq" - the Truth. You and I have a promised reward, and we have the guidelines and our messengers with their practical lives to follow, to make our path easy. Still, where are we heading?

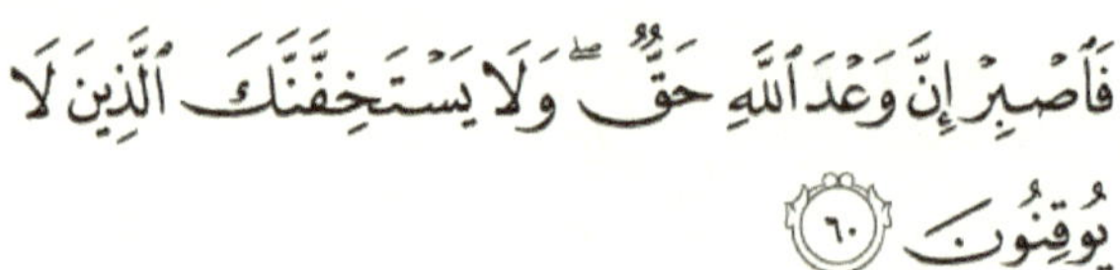

Sahih International
So be patient. Indeed, the promise of Allah (ﷻ), The Exalted, is truth. And let them not disquiet you who are not certain [in faith].
Quran 30:60

Remember, the journey to achieving your Everest Goal is not about reaching the top at all costs; it's about the journey itself. It's about the lessons learned, the challenges overcome, and the personal transformation you undergo. It's about embracing the process, the growth, and the rewards that come with it.

The first ascent is just the beginning. There will be more mountains to conquer, more challenges to overcome, and more milestones to celebrate. But with each step, each hurdle overcome, you become a stronger, more resilient, and more self-aware individual, ready to face whatever comes your way.

My aspiration is to achieve an Everest Goal, but I do not wish to spend only 15-30 minutes at the summit. I dreamed of a peaceful world filled with joy and beautiful souls, surrounded by stunning waterfalls, mountains, and more. I wished to stay there forever and realised my ultimate destination Goal was Jannah. To be in Jannah, to be able to see my Rabb. Once my Goal was set, then it was the preparation and it's a never-ending process, to learn His words, to implement it in my life, to call you all towards it. My book you are reading now is another step of reaching my Everest Goal.

Whatever your goal is, maybe to achieve an educational attainment, to start up a charity organisation, to do your memorisation of the Quran, to seek knowledge of your deen, or whatever it is, start with tiny steps.

The journey towards achieving your Everest Goal is a transformative experience. It's about pushing your limits, embracing challenges, and ultimately discovering the incredible potential that lies within you. It's about finding your inner strength, cultivating resilience, and celebrating the journey as much as the destination.

So, take that first step, set realistic milestones, celebrate your victories, and embrace the journey. You have the power within you to conquer any mountain, and in doing so, you will achieve not only your Everest Goal but also a profound transformation in your life. The journey towards achieving your Everest Goal is a marathon, not a sprint. It's about consistent effort, unwavering dedication, and celebrating the smaller wins along the way. Each step forward, each hurdle overcome, reinforces your belief in yourself and your ability to reach the summit.

Imagine a mountain climber, meticulously preparing for their ascent. They wouldn't simply stroll up the mountain without proper gear, training, and a well-defined plan. Similarly, your journey towards achieving your Everest Goal requires a deliberate approach. This is where setting realistic milestones comes into play. Breaking down your overarching goal into smaller, achievable steps makes the climb less daunting and fosters a sense of accomplishment with each milestone reached.

The Moment

On May 29, 1953, after tireless efforts, they stood victorious at the top of Everest. The world celebrated. Hillary and Norgay had done the unthinkable. They had reached the highest point on Earth, a goal that had eluded climbers for decades.

But their journey was about more than just reaching the top. It was a powerful metaphor for the challenges we all face in life. Just like Hillary and Norgay ran into difficulties, we do too, in our own ways. We hit roadblocks, feel let down, deal with fear and uncertainty, and struggle with self-doubt.

Their story inspires us all. It reminds us that we have an inner strength and resilience that we often forget about. It teaches us to never give up, to work together, and to dream big. Even the toughest challenges can be overcome with determination, commitment, and confidence in ourselves.

Just like Hillary and Norgay, we too can climb our own mountains, overcome our own obstacles, and achieve our own "Everest goals." We can strive for personal and spiritual growth, pushing ourselves beyond our perceived limits, finding strength in adversity, and emerging as stronger, more resilient versions of ourselves. Their story is a beacon of hope, a testament to the human spirit's indomitable nature, a reminder that anything is possible if we dare to dream and believe in ourselves.

Lessons from the Mountains

The tale of Edmund Hillary and Tenzing Norgay's historic ascent, the first to conquer the summit of Everest, is a timeless example of teamwork and perseverance in the face of extreme adversity. Their journey was fraught with challenges – treacherous terrain, unforgiving weather, and the constant threat of altitude sickness. Yet, they never faltered in their commitment, pushing their limits, and supporting each other every step of the way. They relied on their shared expertise and unwavering trust to navigate the perilous climb, proving that a collective effort, guided by a common goal, can achieve the seemingly impossible.

The Icefalls of Fear and Doubt

Fear, often born from uncertainty and the unknown, can paralyse us. It whispers doubts about our capabilities, questioning our ability to succeed. But fear is a deceptive guide. It often exaggerates risks, making us shrink from opportunities that could lead to significant growth. We must acknowledge our fears, recognise them as natural responses, and learn to distinguish real threats from imagined ones. We often get stuck by these fears.

Doubt, a persistent shadow that casts scepticism on our abilities, can erode our confidence. It tempts us to question our decisions, second-guessing our choices and undermining our progress. Doubt can be a powerful force, but it doesn't have to define our journey. We can learn to recognise doubt for what it is: a temporary roadblock, not an insurmountable wall.

Courage, the unwavering determination to face our fears and doubts head-on, is the essential antidote. It's not about being fearless, but about recognising our anxieties and pushing through them. Just as a climber conquers icefalls with a combination of skill and determination, we must cultivate courage as a vital tool in our personal growth.

Think of the countless stories of individuals who have overcome immense obstacles. Think of those, the artists who dared to express their creativity against all odds, and the entrepreneurs who built empires from humble beginnings. Our prophets, in their journey towards establishing the deen of Allah, the exalted.

They faced their own icefalls of fear and doubt, and they found the courage to press on, to persevere, and to ultimately achieve remarkable things.

The journey to achieving our Everest Goals is paved with both triumphs and setbacks. It's a journey of continuous learning, where we face challenges head-on, gain new insights, and ultimately emerge stronger and more resilient.

Imagine a climber struggling against a relentless blizzard, battling blinding snow and bone-chilling temperatures. They are exhausted, their fingers numb with cold, their body aching with exertion. But they do not give up. They know that persistence is their only hope, that quitting is not an option. They dig deep within themselves and find a renewed determination to carry on.

We face similar challenges in our own lives. We encounter setbacks, experience disappointments, and feel the weight of self-doubt. But just as climbers find strength in their shared purpose and unwavering commitment, we too can draw strength from our values, our beliefs, and our unwavering resolve. **The power of the mind plays a crucial role in overcoming** fear and doubt. A negative mindset can amplify our anxieties, feeding self-doubt and creating a vicious cycle of negativity. But a positive mindset can be a powerful tool, empowering us to approach challenges with confidence and resilience.

Shift Your Fear To Submission

From Everest to ocean let me draw you an example. Most of you must know the procedure of "Jettison" (to drop (cargo) to lighten a ship's load in time of distress). When I used to see the documentary of the ship voyage and the documentary on oceans because that's one of my favourite things to learn more about the creations of Allah (ﷻ), The Exalted, I often think about Jettison, the procedure of throwing load overboard. How expensive the load is, but in the situation of heavy storms, the decision is made to "get rid of" to balance the ship. To save your life. Don't you think we too need these Jettisons in our life? Often stuck with loads of burden and grudges and complaints, can't we get rid of - throw off these loads overboard, so that we can balance our thoughts, balance our heart from not getting to rust, not sinking to negative thoughts as the ship would sink and the people will lose their life if they would hold on to the loads thinking, "How could we?"

Storms are again going to hit our life. We can't expect to be happy always. Just as ships do not cease sailing when storms arise, sailors do not fear setting sail once more. That's a step in their journey they take precautions with, such as the one we talked about here - so navigate the ship of your life and confront the storm.

Observe the Birds, they are designed to be lightweight in order to soar to great heights. Keep your heart weightless so you can elevate your positive thoughts. Carrying good things is always a struggle with a heavy heart.

Changing your mindset from fear to belief can have a significant impact. It enables us to access our inner resilience, leverage our own abilities, and face obstacles with a renewed sense of self-assurance.

Overcoming fear and doubt is an ongoing process, not a one-time event. It requires a conscious effort to cultivate courage, to challenge our negative thoughts, and to focus on our strengths. It's about learning to embrace the discomfort of the unknown, to step outside our comfort zones, and to push beyond our perceived limitations.

Fear is an inevitable part of life,

> *"Fear is our survival response," says Northwestern Medicine Clinical Psychologist Zachary Sikora, PsyD.*

In this mode, you need to have complete trust in Allah (ﷻ) that he is going to protect you. That's the belief and strength you need to cultivate. As we went through the stories of our prophets, let me tell you, didn't Musa (Alahi salaam) feel fear when he saw his staff change into a snake? He was talking with Allah, the Exalted. Can you imagine talking to Allah (ﷻ) and feeling fear at seeing the snake, causing him to start running?

وَأَلۡقِ عَصَاكَۚ فَلَمَّا رَءَاهَا تَهۡتَزُّ كَأَنَّهَا جَآنّٞ وَلَّىٰ مُدۡبِرٗا وَلَمۡ يُعَقِّبۡۚ يَٰمُوسَىٰ لَا
تَخَفۡ إِنِّي لَا يَخَافُ لَدَيَّ ٱلۡمُرۡسَلُونَ ١٠

Sahih International
And [he was told], "Throw down your staff." But when he saw it writhing as if it were a snake, he turned in flight and did not return. [Allah (ﷻ), The Exalted said], "O Moses, fear not. Indeed, in My presence the messengers do not fear.

Quran 27:10

And then when Allah, the Exalted, asked to go to Firawn with His message again, Musa (Alayhi Salaam) (PBUH) had the fear of facing the tyrant. Perhaps he may attempt to kill Musa (Alayhi Salaam) (PBUH). But what Allah, the Exalted, said,

Sahih International
[Allah (ﷻ), The Exalted] said, "Fear not. Indeed, I am with you both; I hear and I see."

Quran 20:46

Similarly, we may face many of such situations. Our fear may be sometimes facing the people, sometimes reacting against the evil in front of us, sometimes correcting our loved ones. But always remember the above ayah. It's not only for Musa (Alahi salaam) but for us as well. Hold on with your Lord, and He will take care of you.

- **Mindfulness and Self-awareness:** Taking time to observe our thoughts and emotions, recognising when fear and doubt are taking hold.
- **Positive Self-talk:** Replacing negative thoughts with affirmations that boost our confidence and reinforce our abilities.

- **Goal Setting:** Breaking down our goals into smaller, more manageable steps makes progress seem less daunting. For example, if you need to memorise the Quran, take small steps and be consistent.
- **Visualisation:** Creating vivid mental images of ourselves achieving our goals, building positive expectations, and strengthening our belief. My teacher once said, "When you go to bed, just imagine yourself in paradise. That will boost you for your next day Ibaadah."
- **Support Systems:** Surrounding ourselves with supportive friends, family, and mentors who believe in our potential and offer encouragement along the way.

Our Prophet (PBUH) clearly shows us how our companions must be.

Abu Musa (Alahi salaam) reported: ***The Prophet, peace and blessings be upon him, said, "Verily, the parable of good and bad company is that of a seller of musk and a blacksmith. The seller of musk will give you perfume, you will buy some, or you will notice a pleasant smell. As for the blacksmith, he will burn your clothes, or you will notice a bad smell."***

Source: Sahih al-Bukhari 5534, Sahih Muslim 2628

The journey to overcoming fear and doubt is a journey of self-discovery and transformation. It's a journey that demands courage, determination, and a willingness to embrace the challenges that lie ahead. But it's also a journey that leads to extraordinary growth, self-awareness, and the realisation of our true potential.

Just as the majestic peaks of Everest beckon climbers to push their limits, our own Everest Goals inspire us to strive for greater heights. By conquering the icefalls of fear and doubt within, we pave the way to achieving extraordinary things, not only in our own lives but in the world around us.

The Avalanche of Setbacks

Setbacks are an inevitable part of any journey, and the path to achieving your Everest Goal is no exception. Just as climbers on Mount Everest face treacherous conditions, avalanches, crevasses, and unforeseen challenges, we too encounter obstacles, failures, and setbacks in our own lives. However, the true measure of our resilience and character lies not in avoiding these obstacles, but in our ability to rise above them, learn from them, and emerge stronger on the other side.

Life's setbacks can serve as valuable lessons, pushing us to adapt, innovate, and emerge stronger. When faced with a career setback, a personal loss, or a difficult relationship, it's easy to feel discouraged and question our path. But instead of succumbing to negativity, we can choose to view these challenges as opportunities for growth and transformation.

Think of these setbacks as the 'avalanche of growth.' Just as an avalanche can reshape the landscape of a mountain, setbacks can have a profound impact on our lives, forcing us to re-evaluate our priorities, refine our strategies, and ultimately become more resilient and adaptable individuals.

Here's how to embrace the avalanche of setbacks:

- **Reframe your Perspective:** Instead of viewing setbacks as failures, see them as opportunities for learning and growth. Ask yourself, "What can I learn from this experience? How can I use this challenge to become stronger and wiser?"
- **Embrace Adaptability:** Life is full of surprises, and the ability to adapt is essential for navigating challenges. Be willing to adjust your plans, re-evaluate your strategies, and embrace new approaches.
- **Focus on Resilience:** Building resilience is a lifelong process. Develop a strong sense of self-belief, cultivate a positive mindset,

and surround yourself with supportive relationships. Remember that you are capable of overcoming adversity.

- **Learn from your mistakes:** Every setback presents an opportunity to learn and grow. Take the time to analyse what went wrong, identify areas for improvement, and develop a plan for moving forward.

Embrace the journey:

Remember that the journey to achieving your Everest Goal is not a straight path. It will inevitably have its twists and turns, its ups and downs.

Embrace the process, learn from your setbacks, and keep moving forward with resilience and determination. As my teacher always says, **"Jannah is not for free. You need to work for it..."**

The Thin Air of Self-Sabotage

The biggest blockage of our heart. We all have that inner voice, that nagging critic, that whispers doubts and anxieties. It's the voice that tells us we're not good enough, that we're not capable of achieving our dreams. It's the voice that encourages us to procrastinate, to avoid challenges, to settle for mediocrity. This voice is the embodiment of self-sabotage, a subtle and insidious enemy that can undermine even the most ambitious plans.

This is the biggest trick of Shaytan. He whispers to you, "You are not worth enough. You are sinful. Allah (ﷻ) may not forgive you as you have gone astray." But remember what Allah (ﷻ) says,

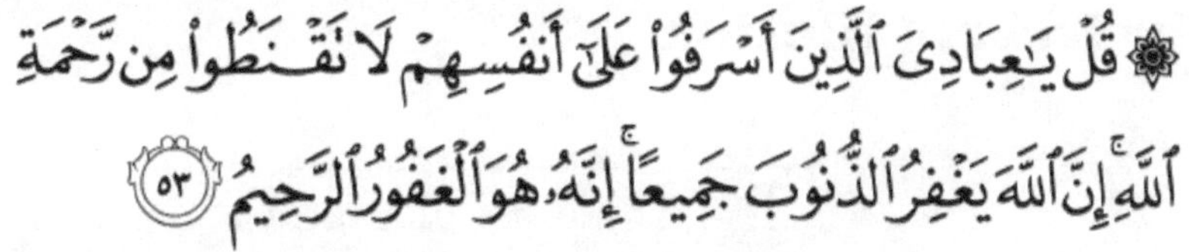

Sahih International
Say, "O My servants who have transgressed against themselves [by sinning], do not despair of the mercy of Allah (ﷻ), The Exalted. Indeed, Allah (ﷻ), The Exalted forgives all sins. Indeed, it is He who is the Forgiving, the Merciful."

Self-sabotage manifests in many ways, but some of the most common traps include:

1. **Procrastination:** We've all been there. We put off tasks, we postpone deadlines, and we make excuses for why we can't get started. Procrastination isn't just laziness; it's often a symptom of fear, doubt, or a lack of self-belief. It's easier to put things off than to face the possibility of failure.
2. **Negative Self-Talk:** The relentless inner critic can be a powerful force. It's the voice that constantly belittles us, telling us we're not smart enough, talented enough, or worthy enough. This negativity erodes our confidence, hindering our ability to pursue our goals.
3. **Lack of Self-Belief:** Perhaps the most significant obstacle to success is a lack of belief in ourselves. We may have dreams and ambitions, but if we don't believe we can achieve them, we're unlikely to even try. Self-doubt can paralyse us, preventing us from taking the necessary steps to realise our potential. Overcoming these traps of self-sabotage requires a conscious effort to shift our mindset and cultivate a more positive and empowering inner dialogue.

The Iceberg Illusion

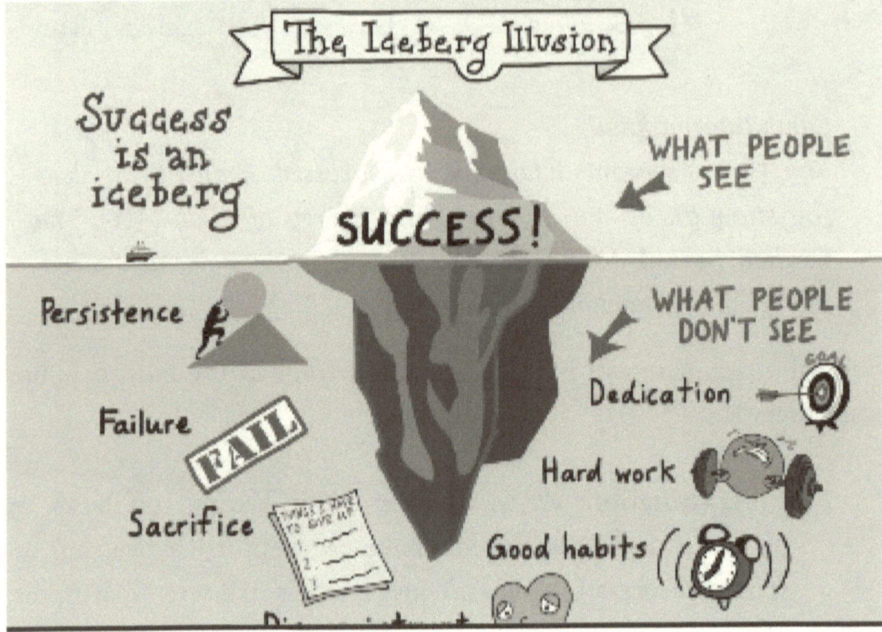

It was when my teacher explained the importance of maintaining consistency in our study routine. She gave us an explanation of the "Iceberg Illusion". Many of you are likely already familiar with this, but I'm including it here as a reminder. The concept of the "Iceberg Illusion" suggests that success is frequently only visible on the surface. The iceberg has two parts: one visible above the water and another larger part hidden beneath the ocean. Likewise, we humans often focus solely on the outward aspect of success. We observe others' achievements and simply feel disheartened by our own lack of success. Success doesn't come without putting in effort. But we overlook the struggles, the setbacks, and effort that were essential to reach that point. It's a beautiful product crafted with lots of effort. Rome wasn't built in a day, right?

The Ultimate Destination - Prepare for it

As we approach the end of this journey, I must remind us both to prepare for the ultimate destination. A day will come, whether it's the next hour, day, year, or even years from now, when we must leave behind all that we have accumulated. In that moment, we will depart with the good we have done. No wealth, no children, no spouse, no parents - none will accompany us. We will be alone, utterly alone.

Anas ibn Malik reported: The Messenger of Allah, peace and blessings be upon him, said, "Three things follow a deceased person. Two of them return and one remains. His family, his wealth, and his deeds follow him. **His family and wealth return, but his deeds remain.**"

Source: Sahih al-Bukhari 6149, Sahih Muslim 2960

Be wise in preparing your eternal life. Don't get deluded with the life of this world. As the life of the world, it will perish one day. As for the eternal life, it's the actual life coming ahead and has no end to it. So be wise in making choices because there is not going to be a second chance. You are never going to come back to patch up the works unfinished.

One of the most notable figures in history, Alexander the Great, was an iconic figure who historically is known for creating an incredibly large empire that stretched from Macedonia to Egypt and other places. Not only did he manage to conquer thousands of cities in the ancient world, but he is also known for spreading scientific thought throughout his empire, ranging from science to mathematics.

These are the words when death approached Him.

I want the best doctors to carry my coffin to demonstrate that, in the face of death, even the best doctors in the world have no power to heal. I want the road to be covered with my treasure so that everybody sees that material wealth acquired on earth stays on earth.

The Messenger of Allah (ﷺ) said, "When a man dies, his deeds come to an end except for three things: Sadaqah Jariyah (ceaseless charity); knowledge which is beneficial, or a virtuous descendant who prays for him (for the deceased)."

Reference: Riyad as-Salihin, 1383

Define your Everest goal and work towards it. If not now, then when?

Remember, life is not about reaching a destination and stopping. It's about the journey, the constant growth, the continuous pursuit of fulfillment. So, embrace the unknown with the confidence of a seasoned climber. Trust your instincts, rely on the strength you've cultivated, and know that you are capable of achieving anything you set your mind to. The summit may be different, your goals may be different from mine, but your inner spirit, your resilience, and your purpose will remain the same.

You've climbed the mountain, now it's time to work towards your goal. You've conquered the Everest within, now it's time to embrace the endless possibilities of life. The journey continues, the ascent never truly ends. And with every new summit, with every new challenge, you become stronger, wiser, and more capable of achieving your dreams.

DETOXIFICATION

It was Mary's painful need that made the infant jesus
Begin to speak from the cradle.
Whatever grew has grown for the sake of those in need,
So that a seeker might find the thing she sought.
If God most High has created the heavens,
He has created them for the purpose of satisfying needs.
Wherever a pain is, that's where the cure goes;
Wherever poverty is, that's where provision goes.
Wherever a difficult question is,
That's where the answer goes;
Wherever a ship is, water goes into it.
Don't seek the water; increase your thirst,
So water may gush forth from above and below.
Until the tender- throated babe is born,
How should the milk for it
Flow from the mother's breast?

– *Rumi*

It is now time for "Detox" - a term commonly used nowadays. How can you cleanse your soul?

During the journey, we have discovered our most valuable possession - our heart. This is the principal aim of cleansing our soul. Always maintain a positive mindset and good intentions in your heart. Do not bring any garbage with you. Write down on a piece of paper all the memories that cause you pain and then burn it. When the paper has burned completely, allow your heart to do the same with those memories. We don't want any memories to be left there that will be a stain. We require our heart to gleam like a diamond - a heart that is refined and resilient.

Surround yourself with righteous and positive individuals who speak kindly, and you will be reminded of Allah, the Most High, who genuinely cares about you. Frequently, we become fond of certain relationships that are harmful to our well-being. If you find yourself in a toxic environment or surrounded by toxic people, remove yourself from that situation. Never confuse putting up with toxic culture with practicing patience.

Having patience does not mean accepting a toxic culture and simply saying "I have patience." In reality, Islam instructs us to condemn what is wrong and promote what is right.

Once the milk goes bad, it becomes curd, which then transforms into paneer, a more costly product. Just like our struggles and challenges, they ultimately lead to something valuable. We grow in strength with every challenge. Have faith in Allah, The Most High.

Shakir
They believe in Allah and the Last Day, and they ***enjoin*** *what is right and forbid what is wrong and hasten to* ***good*** *deeds. And those are among the righteous. Quran 3:114*

يُؤْمِنُونَ بِاللَّهِ وَالْيَوْمِ الْآخِرِ وَيَأْمُرُونَ بِالْمَعْرُوفِ
وَيَنْهَوْنَ عَنِ الْمُنْكَرِ وَيُسَارِعُونَ فِي الْخَيْرَاتِ وَأُولَٰئِكَ مِنَ
الصَّالِحِينَ ﴿١١٤﴾

I appreciate all of you for being part of this amazing adventure and apologise if any of my words hurt you in any way. You are special, you are fantastic, you are strong.

I'm now signing off and wishing all of you good health and a peaceful life, and also praying that Allah (ﷻ) brings us all together in Jannah. Ameen

Alhamdulillah

Notes

* * *

Chapter 1

Rumi quotes -

https://legacy.quran.com/16

https://www.linkedin.com/pulse/steve-jobs-last-words-must-read-every-human-being-chris-surel

Rumi collection Edited by Kabir Helminski

https://www.nytimes.com/2015/05/10/opinion/sunday/judith-shulevitz-mom-the-designated-worrier.html#:~:text=Sociologists%20sometimes%20call%20the%20management,on%20top%20of%20it%20all.

Chapter 2

https://legacy.quran.com/16

https://www.who.int/news-room/fact-sheets/detail/suicide

Rumi collection Edited by Kabir Helminski

Chapter 3

https://matwprojectme.org/ali-banat
https://www.bruneinewsgazette.com/gaza-mothers-face-mothers-day-amidst-ongoing-conflict/
https://www.youtube.com/watch?v=6rnYBvo6cLM- The interview with Ms. Alphia James.
https://legacy.quran.com/16
Rumi collection Edited by Kabir Helminski

Chapter 4

https://www.fao.org/newsroom/detail/un-report-global-hunger-SOFI-2022-FAO/en
https://www.npr.org/sections/goatsandsoda/2016/01/20/463710330/what-happens-to-the-body-and-mind-when-starvation-sets-in
https://legacy.quran.com/16
Rumi collection Edited by Kabir Helminski

Chapter 5

https://legacy.quran.com/16
Rumi collection Edited by Kabir Helminski
https://www.goodreads.com/quotes/4195706-in-compassion-and-grace-be-like-the-sun-in-concealing

Chapter-6

https://legacy.quran.com/16
Rumi collection Edited by Kabir Helminski
https://pmc.ncbi.nlm.nih.gov/articles/PMC8445775/
Chapter-7
https://legacy.quran.com/16
Rumi collection Edited by Kabir Helminski
https://www.abuaminaelias.com/dailyhadithonline/2019/08/18/mercy-greater-than-my-sins/

Chapter 8

https://legacy.quran.com/16

Rumi collection Edited by Kabir Helminski

Ref - https://www.kalamullah.com/Books/Stories%20Of%20The%20Prophets%20By%20Ibn%20Kathir.pdf- The stories of prophets - Al Imam ibn kathir.

https://www.abuaminaelias.com/dailyhadithonline/2012/08/08/allah-more-merciful/

Chapter 9

https://legacy.quran.com/16

Rumi collection Edited by Kabir Helminski

https://www.gaia.com/article/mysteries-of-the-human-heart

men and the universe Reflection of Ibn Al Qayyum By Abdul Hameed Al Qoz Translated into English by Dr.Abdul- Latif Al khaiat

https://www.mountsinai.org/health-library/supplement/dehydroepiandrosterone#:~:text=Dehydroepiandrosterone%20(DHEA)%20is%20a%20hormone,steadily%20as%20you%20get%20older.

https://www.abuaminaelias.com/forty-hadith-purification-of-the-heart/

https://www.abuaminaelias.com/dailyhadithonline/2017/10/11/dua-bring-our-hearts-together/

Chapter 10

https://legacy.quran.com/16

Rumi collection Edited by Kabir Helminski

Mr. Beck weathers " Left for Dead"

Into the Thin Aor - by Jon Krakauer

Quran Images all courtesy to https://legacy.quran.com/16

https://www.tranquilkilimanjaro.com/sir-edmund-hillary-and-tenzing-norgay-the-first-persons-to-climb-to-the-summit-of-mount-everest/?srsltid=AfmBOooahFEMMr8sfH5Nsl6Ir3NY2vvE2RzLobLPzNEIs_GHyXHEFRFUhttps://www.nm.org/healthbeat/healthy-tips/emotional-health/5-things-you-never-knew-about-fear

https://www.thellabb.com/the-iceberg-illusion/

https://www.hughsnews.com/newsletter-posts/the-last-wishes-of-alexander-the-great-by-the-honorable-allen-b-clark-contributing-writer-for-hughs-news

www.ingramcontent.com/pod-product-compliance
Lightning Source LLC
LaVergne TN
LVHW041111150826
845673LV00007B/2006